Stephen Henry Bradbury

Lyrical Fancies

Stephen Henry Bradbury

Lyrical Fancies

ISBN/EAN: 9783744776141

Printed in Europe, USA, Canada, Australia, Japan

Cover: Foto ©Thomas Meinert / pixelio.de

More available books at **www.hansebooks.com**

November, 1865.

A LIST OF BOOKS

PUBLISHED BY MESSRS.

EDWARD MOXON & CO., DOVER STREET.

"The power of English Literature is in its Poets."

Essays on Criticism, by Matthew Arnold.

ANNOUNCEMENTS.

A Selection from the Works and Letters of Charles Lamb,

Prefaced by his Life. By BRYAN W. PROCTER, Esq. (BARRY CORNWALL).

Lyrical Fancies.

By S. H. BRADBURY (Quallon).

[*In December.*

Athenäis.

In small 8vo,

By *WILLIAM STIGANT.*

[*In December.*

Lancelot; and other Poems.

By *W. FULFORD, M.A.*,
Pembroke Coll., Oxford.

Poems by the late Edmund J. Armstrong.

Of Trinity College, Dublin.

[*In November.*

A Biography of William Henry Hunt.

By F. G. STEPHENS.

Illustrated by Chromo-lithographs and Woodcuts of that Artist's Works.

A new and revised edition of

Frances-Anne Kemble's Poems,

Together with some never before published.

Cowl and Cap, and other Poems.
By CATHERINE H. MACREADY.
[In November.

See-Saw; a Novel.
By FRANCESCO ABATI.
Edited by W. WINWOOD READE.

ANNOUNCEMENTS—*continued.*

ILLUSTRATED WORKS.

In foolscap 4to, elegantly printed and bound,
Enoch Arden.
By ALFRED TENNYSON.
Illustrated by 20 drawings on wood by ARTHUR HUGHES.
[At Christmas.

Shortly, in foolscap 4to, antiquely bound, a new edition of
The Princess.
By ALFRED TENNYSON.
With 26 illustrations on wood; engraved by DALZIEL, GREEN, THOMAS, and WILLIAMS, from Drawings by DANIEL MACLISE, R.A.

Shortly, in foolscap 4to, in elegant cloth, a new edition of
The Works of John Keats.
With a Memoir by LORD HOUGHTON. Illustrated by 120 designs by G. SCHARF, F.S.A.

Shortly, in foolscap 4to, bevelled cloth,
Tupper's Proverbial Philosophy.
Which, in addition to drawings by

C. W. COPE, R.A.,	JOHN GILBERT,
FRED. R. PICKERSGILL, A.R.A.,	JAMES GOODWIN,
JOHN TENNIEL,	WILLIAM HARVEY,
EDWARD H. CORBOULD,	J. C. HORSLEY,
GEORGE DODGSON,	WILLIAM L. LEITCH,
EDWARD DUNCAN,	JOSEPH SEVERN,
BIRKET FOSTER,	WALTER SEVERN,

And the Ornamental Initials and Vignettes by HENRY NOEL HUMPHREYS, will contain some entirely new and important illustrations.

Published by Messrs. Edward Moxon & Co.

In foolscap 8vo, price 7s. cloth,

The Romance of the Scarlet Leaf, and other Poems.

With adaptations from the Provençal Troubadours.

By *HAMILTON AÏDÉ*,
Author of "Mr. and Mrs. Faulconbridge," "Rita," &c.

"It is refreshing to meet with strains that flow in grace and music from a generous inspiration."—*Athenæum*, July 29, 1865.

"Careful and graceful verse."—*Examiner*, August 5, 1865.

"They are agreeably and elegantly written."—*London Review*, May 20, 1865.

"Mr. Hamilton Aïdé, who has written one or two very good novels, now publishes some poetry."—*Press*, June 3, 1865.

"His refinement and delicacy are seen to equal advantage, whilst a manliness of tone and a liberality of thought are superadded."—*Reader*, June 6, 1865.

In foolscap 8vo, price 10s. 6d. cloth,

Ephemera.

By *HELEN and GABRIELLE CARR*.
Illustrated by HELEN CARR.

"Marked by a peculiar chastened tone of taste and feeling."—*Athenæum*, July 29, 1865.

"Both ladies write with grace, feeling, and address: not a few of the verses have the true poetical ring."—*London Review*, July 29, 1865.

"Awaken respect for their quality, learning, and engaging melody."—*Public Opinion*, July 29, 1865.

"Under the above *noms de plume* two most talented ladies have published a series of Poems which will be read with pleasure by all who can appreciate imagery flowing out of a fine and original fancy."—*Lord W. Lennox in the Sporting Magazine*, July 29, 1865.

Demy 8vo, elegant cloth, price 9s.,

Studies in Biography.

By *LIONEL JAMES TROTTER*,
Late Captain, 2nd Bengal Fusileers.

"Captain Trotter writes with good sense; his style is pleasing and the work is decidedly interesting."—*Daily News*, August 31, 1865.

"Captain Trotter writes gracefully, and with a fresh appreciation of the great men whose character he discusses."—*Examiner*, April 1, 1865.

"We are able to speak favourably of these essays."—*London Review*, May 20, 1865.

"Much information collected and considerable light thrown upon the important historical eras, the principal events of which were directed by the illustrious persons of whom Captain Trotter has given the biography."—*Press*, Jan. 28, 1865.

"Clever and thoughtful volume of essays."—*Allen's Indian Mail*, April 22, 1865.

"Captain Trotter has a ready pen and a keen appreciation of character."—*Notes and Queries*, Jan. 21, 1865.

MOXON'S MINIATURE POETS.

"'Moxon's Miniature Poets' is the name under which some admirable selections from our recent poetry are now offered to the world."—*Times*, June 6, 1865.

I.

Royal 16mo, toned paper, most elegantly bound and printed,

A Selection from the Works of Alfred Tennyson, D.C.L.,

POET LAUREATE.

With a Portrait of the Author, from a photograph taken by the Stereoscopic Company in November, 1864.

Cloth bevelled, 5s. ; ditto, gilt edges, 6s. ; morocco gilt, 10s. 6d. ; best levant morocco, 21s.

"We can now carry about with us the best pieces of Tennyson in a small pocket volume."—*Times*, June 6, 1865.

"Contains many of Mr. Tennyson's best known, and some of his most splendid efforts."—*London Review*.

"Is an interesting volume in many ways."—*Fortnightly Review*, Oct. 1, 1865.

A Selection from the Works of Robert Browning.

With a New Portrait engraved by J. H. Baker, from a photograph by W. Jeffrey.

Cloth bevelled, 5s. ; ditto, gilt edges, 6s. ; morocco gilt, 10s. 6d. ; best levant morocco, 21s.

"His erudition is very valuable, and gives rich flavour to his sentiment."—*Times*, Jan. 11, 1865.

"He has qualities such as should be cherished by the age we live in, for it needs them."—*Quarterly Review*, July, 1865.

"We have read this selection with real pleasure, and have no hesitation in saying that the author justly ranks as one of the real great poets who, perhaps, has but only one living equal in breadth, comprehensiveness, and subtlety."—*Public Opinion*, October 21, 1865.

III.

A Selection from the Poems of Frederick Locker.

With Portrait by MILLAIS, and 19 Illustrations by RICHARD DOYLE. Price 10s. 6d. elegant cloth.

" . . . Mr. Frederick Locker, who now follows in the wake of the Laureate and of Mr. Browning, has a genuine poetical gift. . . . Leaves a favourable impression of his powers on the minds of all its readers."—*Times*, June 6, 1865.

"Mr. Locker can write vigorously and affectingly."—*Athenæum*, June 17, 1865.

"A very pretty edition of very pleasant rhymes."—*Spectator*, July 1, 1865.

"His epigrams are keen and bright and the jokes good."—*Pall Mall Gazette*, June 15, 1865.

"Mr. Locker writes agreeable *vers de société*, which are to poetry and its searching accents what the pleasant chat of a 'drum' is to the graver conversation of the fireside."—*Fortnightly Review*, July 1, 1865.

"They are pleasantly cynical, agreeably melancholy, full of quaint reflection, and always admirable in their variety and versatility of rhyme."—*Morning Star*, June 12, 1865.

"No unworthy candidate for public esteem and long remembrance."—*Public Opinion*, July 22, 1865.

"He has humour, sprightliness, and elegance."—*London Review*, June 10, 1865.

"One of the prettiest books of the year, both as to get up and otherwise."—*Illustrated London News*, June 10, 1865.

"Mr. Locker's poems have often received in these columns the praise they deserve."—*Press*, July 8, 1865.

"Mr. Locker obviously asks with Horace
        '. . . 'ridentem dicere verum
                Quid vetat?'
and masks many a deep thought and much true poetic feeling under the quips and cranks and wreathed smiles of a wearer of motley."—*Notes and Queries*.

IV.

A Selection from the Poems of William Wordsworth.

Poet Laureate. Edited and prefaced by FRANCIS TURNER PALGRAVE. With Portrait. [*In November.*

V.

A Selection from the Works of Martin F. Tupper, M.A., D.C.L., F.R.S.

With Portrait. [*In December.*

A Selection from the Poems of Percy Bysshe Shelley.

Edited and prefaced by ROBERT BROWNING. With Portrait.

A Selection from the Poems of John Keats.

Edited and prefaced by ROBERT BUCHANAN. With Portrait.

To be succeeded by other equally important Selections from the works of the late THOMAS HOOD, PRAED, WALTER SCOTT, &c., which will be duly announced.

WORKS BY THE LATE S. T. COLERIDGE.

Coleridge's Poems.

A NEW EDITION. In one volume, foolscap 8vo, price 6s. cloth.

⁎ THE ONLY AUTHORISED AND COMPLETE EDITION OF THESE POEMS.

Coleridge's Dramatic Works.

A NEW EDITION. In one volume, foolscap 8vo, price 6s. cloth.

Coleridge's Aids to Reflection.

TENTH EDITION. In one volume, foolscap 8vo, price 6s. cloth.

Coleridge's Friend.

A SERIES OF ESSAYS, TO AID IN THE FORMATION OF FIXED PRINCIPLES IN POLITICS, MORALS, AND RELIGION, WITH LITERARY AMUSEMENTS INTERSPERSED. FIFTH EDITION. In two volumes, foolscap 8vo, price 14s. cloth.

⁎ "This, the *only* authorized edition, is a careful reprint from that edited in 1837, *with the Author's corrections and additions*, by his accomplished nephew, Henry Nelson Coleridge. It is, consequently, the only edition extant which exhibits "The Friend" as left by the author for posterity."—*Rev. D. Coleridge, in a letter to the Publishers.*

Coleridge's Essays on His Own Times.

In three volumes, foolscap 8vo, price 18s. cloth.

Coleridge on the Constitution of Church and State.

FOURTH EDITION. In one volume, foolscap 8vo, price 5s. cloth.

Coleridge's Lay Sermons.

THIRD EDITION. In one volume, foolscap 8vo, price 5s. cloth.

Coleridge's Confessions of an Enquiring Spirit.

FOURTH EDITION. In one volume, foolscap 8vo, price 4s. cloth.

Coleridge's Notes on English Divines.

In two volumes, foolscap 8vo, price 12s. cloth.

Coleridge's Notes, Theological, Political, and Miscellaneous.

In one volume, foolscap 8vo, price 6s. cloth.

Shortly.

Hartley Coleridge's Poems.

In one volume, foolscap 8vo.

An Index to "In Memoriam."

In which every separate clause is referred to under the headings of one or more of the principal words contained in it. Price 2s. cloth limp, or 1s. 6d. sewed, for binding with "In Memoriam."

Conolly's (Dr. John) a Study of Hamlet.

Foolscap 8vo, price 5s. cloth.

"To readers, spectators, and actors alike.... Dr. Conolly's speculations may be very valuable."—*Saturday Review*, July 4th, 1863.

HAYDN'S DICTIONARY OF DATES.

ELEVENTH EDITION. In one volume, demy 8vo, price 18s. cloth; in calf, 24s.,

Haydn's Dictionary of Dates.

RELATING TO ALL AGES AND NATIONS: FOR UNIVERSAL REFERENCE;

Comprehending Remarkable Occurrences, Ancient and Modern—the Foundation, Laws, and Governments of Countries—their Progress in Civilisation, Industry, Literature, Arts, and Science—their Achievements in Arms—their Civil, Military, and Religious Institutions, and particularly of the British Empire. By JOSEPH HAYDN. ELEVENTH EDITION, revised and greatly enlarged by BENJAMIN VINCENT, Assistant Secretary and Keeper of the Library of the Royal Institution of Great Britain.

"15,000 articles all studded with facts as thick as the currants in a Christmas pudding."—*Times*, Nov. 30, 1861.

"'Beware of the man of one book' says the proverb. Certainly we shall beware of the man whose one book is 'Haydn's Dictionary of Dates.'"—*National Society's Report*, Nov. 1862.

THE *LATE* THOMAS HOOD'S WORKS.

Hood's Own.

FIRST SERIES. A NEW EDITION. In one volume 8vo, illustrated by 350 Woodcuts, price 10s. 6d. cloth.

Hood's Own; or, Laughter from Year to Year.

SECOND SERIES. In one volume 8vo, illustrated by numerous Woodcuts, price 10s. 6d. cloth.

Hood's Poems.

EIGHTEENTH EDITION. In one volume, foolscap 8vo, price 7s. cloth.

Hood's Poems of Wit and Humour.

FOURTEENTH EDITION. In one volume, foolscap 8vo, price 5s. cloth.

Hood's Whims and Oddities.

IN PROSE AND VERSE.

With 87 Original designs. A NEW EDITION. In one volume, foolscap 8vo, price 5s. cloth.

Illustrated with a Portrait of the Poet, Photographed from the Original Painting by LEWIS by the Stereoscopic Company.

A COMPLETE RE-ISSUE OF
THE WORKS OF THOMAS HOOD,
COMIC AND SERIOUS, IN PROSE AND VERSE,

CONTAINING ALL THE WRITINGS OF THE AUTHOR OF THE

Song of the Shirt,

("Hood's Own," 1st and 2nd series, excepted,)

That can be discovered by the most Careful Research and Inquiry.

In SEVEN *Volumes, small 8vo, price £2 2s., cloth.*

"The plan adopted is the chronological, so that the series will be not only a collection of the Poet's works, but a history of his mind."—*Athenæum,* February 22, 1865.

"Everything calculated to throw light on the development of Hood's genius will be welcome to the public, whom he moved at will to tears or laughter."—*Daily News,* February 24, 1862.

"What an ingenious and whimsical punster was Hood, and what an exquisite lyrist! Fantastic ideas that would never occur to any other man, came naturally to him."—*The Press,* March 15, 1862.

KEATS' POEMS.
―♦―

Keats' Poetical Works.

With a memoir by the Right Hon. the LORD HOUGHTON.

A new and enlarged edition, in one volume, foolscap 8vo, price 5s. cloth.

The Works of Charles Lamb.

In one volume 8vo, with Portrait and Vignette, price 12s. cloth.

CONTENTS:

1. The Letters of Charles Lamb, with a Sketch of his Life. By Sir T. N. TALFOURD.—2. Final Memorials of Charles Lamb; consisting chiefly of his Letters not before published, with sketches of some of his companions. By Sir T. N. TALFOURD.—3. The Essays of Elia.—4. Rosamund Gray, Recollections of Christ's Hospital, Poems, &c.

The Essays of Elia.

In one volume, foolscap 8vo, price 6s. cloth.

In November, fcap. 8vo, cloth, a NEW EDITION of

Atalanta in Calydon.

A TRAGEDY.

By ALGERNON CHARLES SWINBURNE.

"He [Mr. Swinburne] is gifted with no small portion of the all-important Divine fire, without which no man can hope to achieve poetic success; he possesses considerable powers of description, a keen eye for natural scenery, and a copious vocabulary of rich yet simple English. * * * * We must part from our author with cordial congratulations on the success with which he has achieved so difficult a task."—*Times*, June 6, 1865.

"Exhibits a brilliancy of poetic diction, and a power of melody of a very high order."—*Edinburgh Review*, July, 1865.

"Mr. Swinburne is a true poet."—*Pall Mall Gazette*, April 18, 1865.

"No one who reads 'Atalanta in Calydon' can doubt that its author is a poet—a poet of great grace, flexibility, and power of expression."—*Saturday Review*, May 6, 1865.

"When it is said that Mr. Swinburne can write most delicate and harmonious blank verse—and his blank verse is more evenly unexceptionable than his lyrics—all is not said. His English is pure and extremely fluent; his rhythm is graceful and dignified; his lyrics are often melodiously flexible; but, more than this, he possesses an intense and incisive observation of the external aspects of things; his words chisel them out as clearly as in marble."—*Fortnightly Review*.

"Let our readers say whether they often meet with pictures lovelier in themselves or more truly Greek than those in the invocation to Artemis. Many strains equal to that in force, beauty, and rhythmical flow might be cited from the chorus. Those which set forth the brevity of man's life, and the darkness which enfolds it, though almost irreverent in their impeachment of the gods, are singularly fine in expression. * * * * We yet know not to what poet since Keats we could turn for a representation at once so large in its design and so graphic in its particulars; in the noble hyperbole of description, which raises the boar into the veritable scourge of Artemis, there is imagination of the highest kind. * * * * A subject for many a painter to come—a grand word-picture, in which the influence of no contemporary can be traced. In the fervour and beauty of his best passages we find no reflection of any modern writer."—*Athenæum*, April 1, 1865.

"He [Mr. Swinburne] has produced a Dramatic Poem which abounds from the first page to the last in the finest constituents of poetry—in imagination, fancy, feeling, sentiment, passion, and knowledge of the human heart and soul, combined with a dominant mastery over every species of verse, from the stateliest pomp of epic metre to the fluent sweetness of song. Selecting for his subject one of the most pathetic of the ancient Greek legends, and adopting the grand old models of Greek tragedy, Mr. Swinburne has shown himself thoroughly imbued with antique spirit. He is evidently a good scholar, for he prefaces his poem with three pages of Greek verse, addressed to Walter Savage Landor. Association with such a man as Landor is in itself sufficient testimony to the excellence of a writer's scholarship; but mere scholarship alone would not have enabled Mr. Swinburne to write the dramatic poem now before us."—*London Review*, April 8, 1865.

"This is full of true poetry."—*Spectator*, April 15, 1865.

"Let us here, as space allows no more at present, call attention to the lately published 'Atalanta in Calydon' by Mr. Algernon Swinburne, as the most recent attempt in English literature, within the precincts of what we have called the 'higher muse.'"—*Quarterly Review*, October, 1865.

ALSO, BY THE SAME AUTHOR,
Fcap. 8vo, cloth, price 5s.
The Queen-Mother, and Rosamond;
TWO PLAYS.
By ALGERNON CHARLES SWINBURNE.

Fcap. 8vo, cloth,
Chastelard: a Tragedy.
By ALGERNON CHARLES SWINBURNE.
[*In November.*]

SECOND EDITION.
THE POETICAL WORKS OF
Winthrop Mackworth Praed, M.P.
In Two Volumes, foolscap 8vo, price 14s.

(A few copies only on large paper, Roxburghe binding, price 24s.) Illustrated with a Portrait of the Author, engraved by HOLL, after the original miniature by NEWTON.
Prefaced by a Memoir by the Rev. DERWENT COLERIDGE, M.A.

"One of the most charming books for which any writer of our time has furnished material."—*Saturday Review*, Nov. 1, 1862.

"It was in the airy gambols of social wit and fancy that Winthrop Praed was so admirable."—*London Review*, Sept. 10, 1864.

"The remains of a brilliant man."—*Athenæum*, Sept. 10, 1864.

"Nor do we think that the readers of Lord Houghton and Mackworth Praed will doubt that each has left more than one specimen of what will be handed down with that literature which is destined, at no very distant date, to be more than any other the world's literature—as genuine and delightful poetry."—*Quarterly Review*, October, 1865.

SHELLEY'S WORKS.

Shelley's Poems, Essays, and Letters from Abroad.
Edited by *MRS. SHELLEY.*
In one volume, medium 8vo, with Portrait and Vignette, price 12s. cloth.

Shelley's Poetical Works.
Edited by *MRS. SHELLEY.*
In three volumes, foolscap 8vo, price 15s. cloth.

Shelley's Essays, Letters from Abroad.
TRANSLATIONS AND FRAGMENTS.
Edited by MRS. SHELLEY.
In two volumes, foolscap 8vo, price 9s. cloth.

Shelley's Poetical Works.
In one volume, small 8vo, with Portrait and Vignette, price 7s. cloth.

Shelley Memorials:
From authentic sources.
Edited by LADY SHELLEY.
In one volume, crown 8vo, 5s. cloth.

*** The works of the principal poets are constantly kept in the best levant morocco, elegantly tooled from a design by ROBERT DUDLEY, and particularly suitable for Birthday and Christmas gifts. In ordering these, it is necessary to specify "*Moxon's Binding.*"

WORKS BY THE POET LAUREATE.

Poems.
By ALFRED TENNYSON, D.C.L.
SEVENTEENTH EDITION. In one volume, foolscap 8vo, price 9s. cloth.

Maud; and other Poems.
By ALFRED TENNYSON, D.C.L.
SEVENTH EDITION. Foolscap 8vo, price 5s. cloth.

In Memoriam.
SEVENTEENTH EDITION. Foolscap 8vo, price 6s. cloth.

The Princess.
A MEDLEY.
By ALFRED TENNYSON, D.C.L.
THIRTEENTH EDITION. Foolscap 8vo, price 5s. cloth.

Idylls of the King.
By ALFRED TENNYSON, D.C.L.
A NEW EDITION. Foolscap 8vo, price 7s. cloth.

Enoch Arden, etc.
By ALFRED TENNYSON, D.C.L.
Foolscap 8vo, price 6s. cloth.

*** The above Works are always to be had in Morocco Bindings.

Published by Messrs. Edward Moxon & Co.

WORKS BY MARTIN F. TUPPER,
M.A., D.C.L., F.R.S., of Christchurch, Oxford.

Proverbial Philosophy.
By MARTIN F. TUPPER, D.C.L., F.R.S.
Library Edition, post 8vo, cloth, 8s.

Proverbial Philosophy.
Pocket Edition. 18mo, cloth, gilt leaves, 3s. 6d.

Cithara: Lyrical Poems, Old and New.
Small 8vo, cloth, gilt leaves, 7s. 6d.
Bound in elegant cloth, from Designs by W. HARRY ROGERS.

WORKS BY THE LATE WILLIAM WORDSWORTH.
POET LAUREATE.

Just issued, beautifully bound in fancy cloth, a NEW EDITION of

Wordsworth's Poetical Works.
In six volumes, foolscap 8vo, price 30s. cloth.

Wordsworth's Poetical Works.
In one volume, 8vo, with Portrait and Vignette, price 15s. cloth.

*** *The above are the only* COMPLETE *Editions of Wordsworth's Poems.*

Wordsworth's Prelude; or, Growth of a Poet's Mind.
AN AUTOBIOGRAPHICAL POEM.
SECOND EDITION. In one volume, foolscap 8vo, price 6s. cloth.

The Earlier Poems of William Wordsworth.
In one volume, foolscap 8vo, price 6s. cloth.

Select Pieces from the Poems of William Wordsworth.
In one volume, illustrated by Woodcuts, price 6s. cloth, gilt edges.

*** It must be distinctly understood that all editions, other than those published by Messrs. Moxon, are *incomplete*, and unauthorised by the Poet's family. The amended and additional notes, so necessary to the perfect comprehension of the text, were first published in 1857, and are peculiar to the above editions.

Francis Spira; and other Poems.

By THE AUTHOR OF "THE GENTLE LIFE."

Fcap. 8vo, cloth, price 6s.

"The lyrics will probably be favourably regarded by many to whom poetry is not always acceptable."—*London Review,* June 17th, 1865.

"The attributes of Mr. Friswell's verse are exceeding delicacy, high finish, and a vein of quaint yet always attractive humour."—*Sunday Times,* June 22nd, 1865.

Poetry for Gifts and School Prizes.

Pocket Editions. Elegant cloth.

WORDSWORTH'S POETICAL WORKS. In six volumes, price 15s. cloth.

WORDSWORTH'S EXCURSION. Price 3s. 6d. cloth.

KEATS' POETICAL WORKS. With a Memoir by LORD HOUGHTON (R. M. MILNES). Price 3s. 6d. cloth.

COLERIDGE'S POEMS. Price 3s. 6d. cloth.

SHELLEY'S MINOR POEMS. Price 3s. 6d. cloth.

LAMB'S SPECIMENS OF ENGLISH DRAMATIC POETS. In two volumes, price 6s. cloth.

DODD'S BEAUTIES OF SHAKSPEARE. Price 3s. 6d. cloth.

DANA'S SEAMAN'S MANUAL; by the Author of "Two Years before the Mast." Containing: A Treatise on Practical Seamanship, with Plates; a Dictionary of Sea Terms; Customs and Usages of the Merchant Service; Laws relating to the Practical Duties of Master and Mariners. NINTH EDITION, revised and corrected in accordance with the most recent Acts of Parliament, by the late Commodore J. H. Brown, R.N., C.B., Registrar-General of Merchant Seamen. Price 5s. cloth.

GOETHE'S FAUST. TRANSLATED INTO ENGLISH PROSE, with Notes. By A. HAYWARD, Esq., Q.C., EIGHTH EDITION. Price 4s. cloth.

GREENWOOD'S (COLONEL GEORGE) HINTS ON HORSEMANSHIP TO A NEPHEW AND NIECE; OR, COMMON SENSE AND COMMON ERRORS IN COMMON RIDING. A new, revised, and Illustrated Edition. The wood engravings, photographed from life, are illustrative of the management of the reins in accordance with the principles enunciated in the work. One volume, sm. 8vo. Price 6s.

"A new edition of a very good little book."—*Baily's Magazine,* June 1861.

"His remarks throughout, and especially on the management of the reins, are very correct."—*The Field,* May 25th, 1861.

LORD HOUGHTON'S POEMS (R. M. MILNES). Original Edition. In three volumes, foolscap 8vo, price 15s. cloth.

TALFOURD'S DRAMATIC WORKS. ELEVENTH EDITION. In one volume, foolscap 8vo, price 6s. cloth.

BRADBURY, EVANS, AND CO., PRINTERS, WHITEFRIARS.

LYRICAL FANCIES.

BY

S. H. BRADBURY,

(QUALLON.)

LONDON:
EDWARD MOXON & CO., DOVER STREET.
1866.

LONDON:
PRINTED AT THE REGENT PRESS, 55, KING STREET,
REGENT STREET, W.

TO

SHIRLEY BROOKS, ESQ.,

THE ACCOMPLISHED AUTHOR OF "ASPEN COURT,"
"THE SILVER CORD," AND OTHER WORKS
THAT HAVE NOTABLY ENRICHED
ENGLISH LITERATURE—
AS A TOKEN OF PROFOUND RESPECT
FOR HIS BRILLIANT
AND VERSATILE GENIUS,
AND IN GRATEFUL REMEMBRANCE
OF HOURS MADE HAPPY
BY HIS WARM FRIENDSHIP
AND VALUABLE ADVICE,
THIS VOLUME
IS DEDICATED BY HIS SINCERE FRIEND
AND ADMIRER,

THE AUTHOR.

London, Dec. 1st, 1865.

PREFACE.

At the end of this volume will be found extracts from notices of the press of my work published in 1859. To insert notices of such a kind may be objected to by some persons; but it is thought they may serve to guide the judgment of those critics into whose hands my previous volume did not fall.

CONTENTS.

	PAGE
The Lady Vale	1
The Maiden's Laughter	18
Geraldine	20
The Flower in the Book	23
Oh! beautiful Night	25
R. Cobden	27
Sit by my Side	29
Thoughts by Night	31
I shall not tell her Name	33
The Dream	35
Come Again	40
The truest Noble in the Land	42
Summer	44
Frost on the Panes	46
Stay, dear Maiden	48
An Elegy	50
The Artist	53
In Sorrow	58
Her Raven Curls	60
Lady Gertrude	62

CONTENTS.

	PAGE
OUR TOILERS	64
THE MISER AND HIS GOLD	66
A DREAM OF THE FAIRIES	74
A FRAGMENT	77
IN THE VILLAGE LANE	80
THE BIRD IS SINGING IN THE TREE	82
KATE	84
LADY ALICE	86
IN THE AUTUMN OF THE YEAR	88
THE NIGHT BEFORE THE WEDDING MORN	90
TO THE MOON	92
THE STATUES	94
WISHES	97
THE DEAD ONE'S GRAVE	99
TO AURORA	101
IN YONDER COT	103
THE CASTLE BY THE RHINE	105
THE POETRY OF EARTH	108
ADA	110
THE OLD WHEEL IN THE MILL	113
TO JUNE	115
FIRESIDE MUSINGS	117
UNDER THE HOLLY	121
LINES FOR THE POOR	123
LOVE LYRIC	125
A ROSY FACE AND CHESTNUT HAIR	127
IF I SHOULD LEAVE THE EARTH ERE THEE	129
AMID THE CLOVER	131

CONTENTS.

	PAGE
She lives in Heaven	133
What shall I do to Win her Hand	135
Maiden Beauty	137
The Open Window	139
An Epitaph	141
A clear Blue Sky and Golden Moon	144
The Vacant Chair	146
Song	148
The Glory of Labour	150
Twilight Reveries	153
An Evening Scene	155
Beauty	158
Beside the Evening Fire	159
The Maiden's Voice	161
In the Courts and Alleys Born	163
Sitting at the Window	167
On the River	170
Maiden Worship	172
Little Cherub	174
Wasted Days	176
A Dirge	178
The Sleeping Child	180
The Village at Evening	182
Bacchanalian	184
The Storm	185
In her Lone Room	187
The Village School	189
The Worker	191

	PAGE
THE BRIDGE	193
RURAL SKETCH	195
THE BROKEN HARP	198
BESIDE THE BROOK	201
FLORENCE NIGHTINGALE	202
MY COUNTRY	204
THE BATTLE OF BOSWORTH	206
THE PAST	208
AUTUMN	210
TREAD SLOWLY	212
FANCIES	214

THE LADY VALE.

In years gone by a peasant youth
   Was filled with love for Lady Vale.
The daughter of the proudest earl
   That e'er was clad in coat of mail.
He wooed her long with secret words,
   For years his hopings were in vain :
Wild hope, to thrill a peasant's breast,—
   A gay patrician's hand to gain !

Romance was built within his soul,
   And gave deep passions to his dreams ;
Pure thoughts were in his bosom laid
   Like whitest pebbles glassed in streams.
He watched the Lady Vale by noon
   Walk o'er the bridge that spanned the moat,
And saw her like a wave of light
   Step smiling in her gleaming boat.

He saw the boat with gilded sides
    Move on the water with his love;
He saw her oft, half lost 'mong leaves,
    Appear like to a fluttering dove.
Each spot that gave to him a view
    Of one he loved was quickly known:
He gazed upon her as he stood
    Still as a figure formed of stone.

And when he heard her laughter run,
    In lucent luxury, he was made
To feel the wildest throbs of love,
    Among the brightest scenes to wade.
No cord about his heart was still,
    New fancies woke upon his brain;
As placid river's ringed with smiles,
    When lightly struck with drops of rain.

He watched her from the garden paths
    Among the drooping roses walk:
No music ever smote his ears
    So strangely as her merry talk.
A martyr doomed to stand in fire
    Ne'er looked so stern, nor felt so brave;
Upon his heart his purpose lay
    Like turf upon a guarded grave.

He pined to win the Lady Vale,
   Yet she was proud and he was poor ;
As well essay to fling from earth
   To heaven one drop of human gore ;
As well attempt to move the Sphinx,
   Or calm the sea when mad with foam,
As thou, poor peasant youth, to be
   A guest in Lady Vale's proud home.

Poor Juvol ! one of Labour's sons,
   The Lady Vale thy plea would spurn ;
Once fired with love the mind undimmed,
   Unquenched, and beautiful will burn.
Poor peasant Juvol vowed he 'd win
   The Lady Vale to be his bride ;
He thought her heart would ope to him,
   And cherish not one spark of pride.

He looked by night upon the hall
   Where dwelt the Lady Vale, and prayed
That he might but one moment be
   Upon the pathway where she strayed.
Her beauty took his soul a slave,
   And bound him in a golden chain ;
It threw about him magic gleams,
   Like sun-rise through blue-tinted pane,

Skies had to him a ruddier glow
   Than ever they had worn before ;
Life had revealed to him a prize
   That made him idolize—adore.
Night brought him dreams of Lady Vale,
   He kissed her hand and clasped her waist ;
And in her large and liquid eyes
   His own exulting likeness traced.

At eve he saw the lady sit
   On balcony with book in hand ;
Her brow by leaves of lemon trees
   Half hid and touched was faintly fanned.
She gazed upon the book like saint
   From marble wrought by rarest skill ;
And moved not till the moon arose
   White as a diamond o'er the hill.

And when she bowed her lovely head,
   In golden waves her ringlets fell,
And on her heaving bosom lay,
   Moved gently by its snowy swell.
To be then by the lady's side
   Juvol would face a thousand swords ;
He would have drained his eager heart
   Of passion and his mouth of words.

When through the windows of the hall
    The lights a mellow glimmer cast,
He gazed while thoughts of strangest shape
    Upon his mind long-tortured past.
On balcony he would have stood
    And prayed but for one moment's speech :
To be but for a moment placed
    Within the lady's dainty reach.

Rare music slept within her lips,
    It was her prisoner till she spoke ;
Young Juvol listened to the tones,
    Pleased as a child by laughter woke.
He feared to speak lest she might scorn
    The meagre nature of his state ;
One haughty word, one angry look,
    Would fix a brand upon his fate.

One morn he rose with will to dare
    The lady's look and once to speak ;
Strong was the passion in his soul,
    And yet his tongue was ever weak.
The morning broke without one cloud,
    The east was flushed with rosiest hues :
That died away, when through the trees
    The eye caught affluent sapphire views.

Bees hummed about the thymy plots,
   On roses basked, dew-spangled o'er:
He saw the lark from clover rise,
   And bathed in sun-fires skyward soar.
From fields and gardens odours came,
   And fainted on the languid air;
A sculptured form of Venus stood
   Close by the hall with bosom bare.

And statues of great poets too
   Stood proudly ranged in marble rows,
O'er whose undying labours Fame
   Its best and brightest halo throws.
Young Juvol now the garden sought,—
   He knew the spots the lady paced,—
He thought the flowers the sweetest bloomed
   Where most her worshipped presence graced.

He saw her slowly leave the hall,—
   His heart was beating wild and loud;
He watched her moving like the moon
   That breaks the darkness of a cloud.
The path by which he stood she took;
   With fear his frame began to shake,
And locked the language of his tongue,
   And froze the vow he sighed to make.

Ere sped the lady where he stood,
    He dared her glance superb to meet;
He quailed before her azure eyes,
    And knelt in slavery at her feet.
" Forgive me, noblest maid," he spoke,
    " Thy glory has enchained me long;
Thy grace to me is dearer far
    Than richest fancies to a song.

" Thou hast been present night and day
    Unto my soul; and I have seen
More splendour in thy form and face
    Than ever dowered the greatest queen.
I am thy stricken, humble slave;
    Scorn not, spurn not, my honest vow;
More love ne'er filled a human breast
    Than that which fires my bosom now.

" Had I the world it should be thine,
    There is no state I'd hold from thee;
If e'er of captive thou hast dreamed,
    Behold that creature now in me.
Poor is the offering to thy rank,
    And I must die if thou should'st frown;
I would declare my love the same
    Were I the wearer of a crown."

He paused; the lady on him gazed
    Like one who knows not what to speak:
Her will to spurn his simple prayer
    She felt that moment was too weak.
Young Juvol looked up to her face,
    And there a smile of pity played;
It flashed upon his haggard look
    Like sunshine on an unsheathed blade.

The beauty that he 'd long adored
    Now won to tears his eager eyes;
He felt half blinded by her power,
    As though he 'd looked on sun-tinged skies.
A bracelet clasped one rounded arm,
    With rarest jewels sprinkled o'er;
Like to a fading spark of fire
    An opal on her breast she wore.

Her lips like holly berries shone,
    The pink gleam on each cheek would show
As hue of rose on marble shed,
    Or peaches set in glittering snow.
Her dress hung loose in many folds,
    In each there seemed to dwell a grace,
Made by the movement of her form,
    'T were greatest blindness not to trace.

There was large meaning in her eyes,
    For they were Love's unclouded deeps;
There rich desires half hidden lay,
    For there the heart's best likeness sleeps.
The lady's look on Juvol's face
    Soon hurried all his passions up,
As swarm the glimmering globes of wine
    Unto the top of golden cup.

"I am not angry with thee, friend,"
    The lady spoke; in Juvol's ears
The words went shivering to his heart,
    As though 'twere stabbed with hundred spears.
She fixed her glance upon his face,
    And there was kindness in her look;
In which rare pleasure seemed to dwell,
    Like honey-worded song in book.

A radiant smile spread from her lips,
    Unto her cheeks pale dimples came;
Half playful and half proud she asked
    The prostrate Juvol for his name.
There was great witchery in her voice,
    Voluptuous cadence in its tones;
As fresh as babblings of a rill
    That gambols over weeds and stones.

A band of purple velvet ran
    Around her brow, on which were set
A dazzling shower of lucent pearls,
    Like rain-drops flung on violet.
And on her temples, faintly blue,
    The veins were seen like streaks of sky,
Beheld through whitened clouds at eve,
    Whose summits wear a crimson dye.

Young Juvol slowly lisped his name—
    The lady listened, and away
From her poor lover's side she sped—
    The while his heart in sorrow lay.
He set his heart upon her own,
    Like child's on what it cannot reach:
For Love's remorse and shattered dreams
    To life the bitterest lessons teach.

We garner wisdom from the past,
    We learn our morals from our woe;
And half the cares that chequer life
    To pleasure's thoughtless hours we owe.
Poor Juvol's soul was filled with pain;
    He thought the lady's heart was stone,
That it poured not its gladness out
    As full and freely as his own.

He sought his home and wept hot tears,
    Fierce fire was kindled on his brain;
Keen sorrows ran about his thoughts,
    Like lightnings vaulting in the rain.
In dreams the lady near him stood;
    He tried to clasp her, but in vain;
He moved like one whose limbs are bound
    And fettered by a burning chain.

His spirit had no taint of guile,
    He spoke the language that he felt;
No saint more truthful ever prayed,
    Or with more faithful fervour knelt.
Months passed away, and Juvol's hope
    Began to flourish and to rise
Like star that with cool glitter breaks
    At evening in the unmooned skies.

He met the lady near the hall;
    Upon her face a smile was seen,
That told young Juvol where her thoughts,
    Free as the birds in dells, had been.
Once more he dared to speak a word,
    To pour his rapture in her heart;
To watch her eyes from dreamy ease
    To large and lustrous wonder start.

She listened to his simple words,
    And each to her seemed pure and true ;
Around her mind his pleadings ran,
    And into Love's warm glory grew.
She loved to meet him day by day,
    And at the closing of the eve ;
When perfumes from the lilac bloom
    Upon the air faint luxuries leave.

They met when night had strewn her gems
    Upon the grass in gleaming crowds,
That lay like stars, whose silver orbs
    Drop splendour through the swimming clouds.
They walked by rills half hid by flowers,
    And whispered when the zephyrs stirred ;
And vows more earnest from young lips
    The listening angels never heard.

As lightly stepped the Lady Vale
    As snowflake on a frozen stream,
At such dear moments in her eyes
    Her soul seemed palaced in a dream.
Around her waist young Juvol's arm
    Was then so fondly, proudly twined ;
The richness of her silver talk
    Set beauties blooming on his mind.

And when the moon rose, round and pale,
  Pure as great diamond through the dark,
They roamed beneath the elms that threw
  Huge shadows in the level park.
A change came o'er the Lady Vale ;
  Her father learnt her love and frowned ;
And when she dared not leave the hall
  Her fading cheeks in tears were drowned.

In secret she was doomed to pine ;
  Her freedom curbed, her gladness went :
With sorrow she gazed o'er the days
  In love and pleasure she had spent.
Soon for a distant shore she left
  Her father's home ; his anger wore
The nature that, once planted, leaves
  The proud insulted heart no more.

Of Juvol's love she daily dreamed,
  While moving in a foreign land :
For past delights upon the mind
  Like old and broken statues stand.
They are the links that bind the past,—
  Too often forge our keenest ills ;
When sorrow every growing thought
  With wild and secret torture fills.

Alas! poor Lady Vale, thy deeds
    Had not one stain or trace of sin;
'Twas but the opening of thy heart
    For love to gaily flutter in!
Though far away, young Juvol's heart
    Is thine for ever, ever thine;
His tears are shed like June's warm rains
    Upon the juicy fruited vine.

Your minds in wedded compact lived,
    Were sweetly tangled, that no fear
E'er threw a shadow on your lives
    Or drew unto your eyes one tear.
The paths where strayed the Lady Vale
    Seemed lonely, and no laughter rung
In lucid peals through myrtle trees,
    Like bells 'gainst golden vases swung!

She walks not where the chestnut's bloom
    Gives fragrance to the slumberous air,
Nor where green leaves shut from the gaze
    The lovely haunts where ring-doves pair.
And if she glances on the sky,
    Warm tears adown her wan cheeks swim,
As rain-drops down a window pane,
    When day is waning cold and dim.

Years passed away ; her father's hate
    Had not a change—he cursed her name ;
He thought her love a brazen crime,
    To bring disgrace, to end in shame.
Unknown she left her foreign home,
    To meet young-Juvol once again ;
For she was bound unto his soul,
    And threats to daunt her all were vain.

Of her resolve young Juvol heard,
    And yearned to hold her in his arms,
To look once more upon a face,
    That gave his life such mingled charms.
They met once more—the day had gone.
    The white moon flooded all the sky ;
The cool winds to the lilies crept,—
    Stole kisses and then hurried by.

The lady fell in Juvol's arms :
    Few moments thus in silence past :
Her curls upon her shoulders lay,
    Like orient gold on ivory cast.
" 'Tis madness, Juvol, to have loved,
    As I have madly worshipped thee,"
The lady cried ; young Juvol spoke,
    " Thy wrongs are sacred unto me."

From phial filled the lady drank,
   Quaffed eagerly each drop and drain ;
A moment and she lightly fell,
   Upon the turf like drop of rain.
She moved no more—to Juvol's heart
   A thousand horrors winged their way ;
He spoke not, but beside her corpse
   Pale as a murdered hero lay !

Long hours in stupor he was held,
   And when he woke his mind was gone ;
He looked upon the corpse and laughed,
   And cried aloud, " Wake, lovely one."
Ere morning broke his mind again
   Was strong as in the days of yore ;
But all its gladness had died out,
   His look was haggard—young no more.

Then with his hands he made a grave,
   And there the Lady Vale he laid ;
'Twas in a lone sequestered spot,
   Where beams of sunshine never played.
He longed to moulder by her side,—
   Struck near his heart a blade of steel :
He did not care to speak his woes
   Nor that night's horrors to reveal !

And with the warm blood from his breast,
    His lips and hands death-like and pale ;
Upon the cold and dewy turf,
    He wrote " Peace to the Lady Vale."
Then bleeding on the grass he lay,
    Near to his lifeless idol's side ;
Without a shriek—without a groan,
    He closed his wild large eyes and died!

Years have gone by ; the bloody words
    Plain on the turf may yet be seen ;
The grass no longer grows, 't is said,
    Where marks of human blood have been !
For years no eye beheld the grave ;
    At length were found but fleshless bones ;
And now, each midnight, from the spot
    Is heard the sound of human groans !

Old gossips hold the place in awe ;
    To speak its history never fail :
There maids by day oft shed a tear,
    And whisper, " Peace to Lady Vale ! "

THE MAIDEN'S LAUGHTER.

I own it was her laughter
    That won me to her side;
I own I loved the maiden,
    Pale-browed and azure-eyed.
I own the maiden's graces
    First made me yearn to speak;
My love was told in blushes
    From burning brow to cheek.

I own I was her captive,
    When first I saw her smile;
I turned away my glances,
    Yet saw her all the while!
I own her gentle spirit
    First led me to adore—
The softest, sweetest music
    Could not have thrilled me more.

I lived in rarest bondage;
    I lost my heart and hand;
The maiden was my idol,
    The fairest in the land.
Where'er she walked I wandered,
    Alone where she had strayed;
Ne'er for a brighter treasure
    A martyr ever prayed.

The green leaves seemed to whisper
    That she was queen of girls;
E'en zephyrs seemed to loiter,
    For pleasure, 'mong her curls.
Love blossomed in her glances,
    The hours were made to shine:
'T was Nature made her lovely!
    ' Twas love that made her mine!

GERALDINE.

Oh! stately was the lovely Geraldine,
  A picture perfect as she lay asleep;
A brow where glorious intellect was seen;
  Where artist might new thoughts of beauty
      reap.
Arms white as marble, and so sweetly round,
  Bare on the silken coverlet were laid;
Like image of snow-wreaths in lakelet drowned,
  And, hushed in dreams, her lips like rose-
      leaves played.

The faintest pink dwelt on each rounded cheek,
  And to the pillow gave a rosy hue,
Like morning's blush on lilies; eyes might seek
  Its like in crimson tulip filled with dew.
A band of blushing velvet bound her arm,
  With diamonds sprinkled, raining sparks of
      light;
Each violet-coloured vein ran like a charm
  Till they were lost 'mong curls dark as the
      night.

Her bosom wave-like ever rose and fell,
   The coverlet revealed its ample mould ;
The moon ne'er looked so white, seen from a
      dell,
   Nor image fairer could these eyes behold !
And when the morning through her chamber
      blushed,
   It seemed to borrow beauty as it strayed
To where she lay, in silver visions hushed,
   Still as a goddess in a robe arrayed.

And when she rose she laved her beauteous
      form,
   Then in the water plunged, while ripples
      prest
In hurried crowds to dally and to warm,
   To clasp and lie about her heaving breast.
She rises from the bath ; in silken dress
   Made loose and lustrous soon her form appears ;
Then in a sable mass each glossy tress
   Holds in its fragrant coil pearls pale as tears.

With peerless majesty she walks the floor,
   In honeyed accents warbles some sweet strain
By olden poet rich in golden lore,
   With lucent fancies lit like drops of rain.

A full midnight of splendour gleams her eye,
　　Where the attracted sunlight swarms and
　　　　wades ;
And every zephyr, ere it flutters by,
　　Her silken bodice lovingly invades.

Then to her bower she walks with gilded book,
　　Whose leaves are perfumed and whose
　　　　thoughts are rare ;
E'en there stray sunbeams thro' the vine
　　　　leaves look,
　　As though they strove to find an angel there.
More wealth of beauty never touched the earth,
　　Such languaged eyes before were never
　　　　seen ;
No eloquence could ever paint the worth
　　Of peerless, happy-hearted Geraldine !

THE FLOWER IN THE BOOK.

I PLACED a snowdrop in a book
  When bridal spring first came to earth;
I plucked it from a sunny nook,
  And tried in vain to sing its worth.
I placed the treasured book aside,
And wondered when the snowdrop died.
I had no wish to see it dead,
Thoughts told of joys its life had shed.

Days travelled on; the summer came;
  I oped the book and blessed the flower;
It seemed to me like perished fame,
  Born but to glimmer for an hour.
The marble hue that once it bore
Was gone, 'twas withered to the core;
'Twas like a thought that lingers on
The memory when its charm has gone.

I loved it ere I broke the stem
    On which it trembled night and morn ;—
For laughing spring, a fragile gem,
    By south winds kissed, in sunshine born.
A sadness in my soul it made,
I did not wish to see it fade ;
I would have toiled to save its bloom,
By morning's smiles, through nights of gloom.

There is a truth in all dead things
    That subtlest speech can never tell :
'Tis like the sound of folding wings
    Unseen, and clasping like a spell.
That snowdrop dead around the mind
Thoughts of its living beauty twined ;
For scenes of death make thoughts of life,
Things living with dead thoughts are rife !

And like this snowdrop hopes all fade,
    Too transient and too frail to last ;
And when once gone, the charms they made
    Will lead the mind unto the past.
To mourn the loss of early years,
When age upon the mind appears ;
And to the future gives a look,
Like this dead snowdrop in the book.

OH! BEAUTIFUL NIGHT.

Oh! beautiful night,
    Thou art shining still;
What musical tones
    Are made by the rill!
The light of the moon
    Is thrown on the hill.

Most beautiful night,
    Undimmed by a cloud;
In gleaming shoals come
    Thy stars in a crowd;
Like maidens at prayer,
    Lone lilies are bowed!

Rare, beautiful night,
    Thou art not alone;
The moon on thy brow,
    Like a white rose blown:
I call thee my love,
    When evening has flown!

Proud, beautiful night!
    Earth borrows from thee
The moments of peace,
    Far dearest to me,
When prints of thy stars
    Gleam white in the sea!

Cool, beautiful night!
    I gaze on thy skies,
As lover would look
    On maiden's blue eyes;
Thy southern winds soft
    As the faintest sighs.

Calm, beautiful night!
    Dost see human tears,
And number the woes
    Humanity bears,—
The sorrowful look
    Each fallen one wears?

Sweet, beautiful night!
    I worship the hours
Thou givest the world;—
    Thy spirit that dowers,
With a dream of dew,
    The honey-filled flowers!

R. COBDEN.

Gone, gone to earth! we mourn thee now;
In thee the fire of freedom burned;
  We know thy loss—remember how
All wrongs by thee were bravely spurned—
Thy full great mind to goodness turned.

Thy battles for the poor shall make
A deathless chaplet for thy name;
  Death cannot from thy glory take.
'Twill ever proudly glow the same,
The worthiest honour stamped with fame.

  Schooled with the people, all thy power
Was used to help their righteous cause;
  'Twas well that God should richly dower
Thy mind to toil for purest laws,
Winning but heeding not applause.

No rank gave lustre to thy birth,
No lordly heritage was thine;
   Thy virtue proved thy radiant worth—
Thou splendour of a lowly line!
Thy name can never cease to shine.

   Untold the worth of thy bequest
Unto thy country, and it bears
   An endless blessing—take thy rest,
Thou'rt greater now than kings and peers,
Thy name as lasting as the years.

   Death won thee, but thou wilt live on,
Thy works thy valorous history tell:
   There's brightness when the sun has gone;
Thy spirit will among us dwell
Like sound of ocean in the shell.

SIT BY MY SIDE.

Sit by my side, my love of love,
   I'll proudly listen to thy strains;
With me the God Divine this hour
   In calm and perfect beauty reigns.
The mists of care fade from my sight:
   Unlanguaged I look on thy bloom;
It breaks in splendour on my gaze,
   As full moon smites the midnight's gloom.

Thy love to me like beacon burns:
   It clasps me in its gracious power;
Deep in my heart its sweetness lies,
   Like honey draughts in sun-blown flower.
I cannot speak the joy I own
   In presence of that look of thine!
The beauties of thy modest life
   Are glowing round this life of mine.

'Tis love like thine that lures the heart :
    Such love to life its fondness gives ;
It grows in radiance like a blush :
    In rare and rosy perfume lives.
I dream of thee, love, as I walk
    The paths where Labour's sceptre swings,
Where grand as thunder fall its strokes,
    And where its iron music rings.

I walk with thee in proud bright dreams
    When night o'er earth broods dim and calm.
And black clouds blind its azure dome,
    Dark as the shadows of the palm.
'Tis love like thine that leads the heart
    To shun betimes its daily cares ;
That makes its worship as sublime
    As dying saints' or martyrs' prayers !

THOUGHTS BY NIGHT.

The orb of day has gone once more,
   A pensive darkness shrouds the land :
Upon the river and the shore
   Great shadows like black columns stand.
The night seems sad, as though it mourned
   To view the miseries of the crowd ;—
The eyes from Nature's beauties turned,
   The wanton follies of the proud.

I too am sad, yet there's a charm
   In night that I can ne'er explain ;
It clasps me like a loving arm,
   And guides me back to youth again.
When robed in darkness thoughts of earth
   And man and all his troubles rise ;—
How poor the monarch's gilded worth,
   How vain the wisdom of the wise!

Like broken gods, I see through tears,
    The shattered hopes of bygone days:
Some born in rapture, some in fears,
    Now gleaming with but faded rays.
'Tis Age that gives to early dreams
    That sober look which now they bear,
As Autumn shows in meadow streams
    The dying beauty of the year.

I'm led to muse how many hearts
    For some great prize have toiled in vain:
How often death, long-welcomed, starts
    To cool the burning of the brain.
Perchance while musing I behold
    The past grow brilliant as of yore:
'Tis then the mind will ope to hold
    Thoughts of the hearts now young no more.

I SHALL NOT TELL HER NAME.

I know a maid to whom I've paid
   More homage than to fame;
Her rubied mouth
Warm as the South,
   But I shall not tell her name.

Her pretty wiles and sunny smiles
   Oft thrilled me when they came;
Her lips have hues
Like crimson dews,
   But I shall not tell her name.

Her foot is small, her figure tall,
   Her hands the lilies shame;
Each lustrous curl
The zephyrs whirl,
   But I shall not tell her name.

Each eye, though dark, has a golden spark
   That takes a magic aim;
My arm in haste
Has clasped her waist,
   But I shall not tell her name.

Her hair, nut-brown, her shoulders drown
   In splendid waves, the same
As sunbeams thrown
On blossoms blown,
   But I shall not tell her name.

In primrose dells she sings and dwells,
   Her beauty earns her fame;
I'll say I think
Her cheeks are pink,
   But I must not tell her name.

Her brow, I know, is fair as snow,
   And marble has no claim,
With all its charms,
To match her arms,
   But I shall not tell her name.

For she was born, like hues of morn,
   The tints of art to shame;
She lights the shade
That night has made,
   But I shall not tell her name!

Her eyes, ne'er dim, seem made to swim
   In brightness still the same;
Neck white as pearls,
The queen of girls,
   But I will not tell her name.

THE DREAM.

One evening I was weary, and my thoughts were lone and dreary,
As I wandered in the village where the children were at play,
And I saw long dusky shadows thrown upon the emerald meadows,
And a sadness on my spirit, like a crushing burden lay,
While in secret I was praying for my grief to pass away.

I heard the children singing, and their merry laughter ringing
Made me feel that I was lonely, with no cheering prospects near;
Yet I hoped, while pressed with sorrow, for a solace in the morrow,
And prayed that I might borrow from the future hopes to cheer;
That some form of love and beauty, making gladness would appear.

Upon the past I pondered, as alone I slowly wandered,
To descry a place of resting in a cool and flowery dell;
I watched the sun declining, like a burning ruby shining,
Where the chestnut boughs were twining, and it soothed my spirit well;
And each spot was swathed in glory where the sun's effulgence fell.

I lingered heavy-hearted, till the red sun had departed,
In that dell of flowers and dewdrops till night's stillness should come on;
I had no gleam of gladness, but was wedded unto sadness,
While the pale cold hue of madness, dimly on my fancy shone,
Like the feeble spark of taper when its sickly flame has gone.

Quickly in a dream I slumbered, and my woes no longer numbered,
For I saw an angel smiling, walking calmly to my side,

And it whispered, " Lonely mortal! thou hast
    a soul immortal
That may enter Heaven's gold portal, when
    thou'st crossed life's troubled tide :
See'st thou not when fades the tempest, how
    the clouds in brightness ride ?

"The cares by mortals tasted, are reproofs for
    moments wasted,
For the precious treasures squandered, kindly
    laid within their reach ;
It seems that man will never, from his heedless
    pleasures sever,
Blindly facing ruin ever, seeing not that each
    for each
For eternal peace should labour, and the noblest
    duties teach ! "

Then a calm came o'er my spirit, and I thought
    I could inherit,
Once again the joys of childhood, in the happy
    days of yore,
When I had no feelings blighted, and felt each
    moment lighted,
With a rapture no one slighted, when my heart
    a treasure bore,
Beautiful with sunniest glimmers and a warm
    romantic lore.

Then the angel from me vanished, and I felt
 the burden banished
That had filled my soul with anguish, while
 my dream went on sublime;
Men I saw as brethren meeting, each other
 fondly greeting,
Kindest wishes oft repeating, with no trace of
 guile or crime,
Strangers from each toiling kingdom and from
 every state and clime.

As I woke my soul was lighter, and the future
 hovered brighter,
While the shivering stars were crowded, and to
 earth their lustre flowed;
The moon with beauty teeming, with a primrose hue was beaming,
Like a dying maiden seeming, up the dark
 clouds faintly rode
Till the dell where I was walking like a golden
 ocean glowed!

Once again to home I wandered, and on my
 dream I pondered;
Quiet reigned about the village, and each spot
 seemed still and lone;

I'd lost my care and sadness, and a thought of
 love and gladness
Had chased away the madness that had marked
 me for its own.
All the sorrows of the evening through that
 angel's words had flown!

COME AGAIN.

Summer, come again to earth,
    Let me see thy sunny bloom;
Let the crimson rose have birth,
    Winter chills me with its gloom.
Throw thy beauty on the wold,
    Virgin spring will quickly wane;
Give the flowers their hues of gold,
    Let thy sunshine flood the lane.

Wake again the humming bee,
    Toiling 'mong the honeyed flowers;
In my dreams I hear and see
    Once again thy murmuring showers.
Let me see thee gild the hill,
    Warmly in the valley glow;
Watch thy sparkles on the rill
    Where the red, red roses blow.

Whisper round the cowslip's bells,
    Let their odours round me swim;
As I view from leafy dells
    Cloudlets shade the sun's white rim.
Perfumed chestnut blossoms bring,
    Dewy morns and skies of blue,
When with birds the woodlands ring:
    Vernal heavens of sun and dew.

Come again, dear Summer, soon;
    Show once more thy green, green leaves;
Send the purple-hearted June,
    With its flushed and mellow eves.
Earth in thy warm kisses shines,
    Quaffs thy cool delicious showers,
For thy gentle coming pines,
    At thy touch she laughs in flowers.

Like a lover unto thee
    I am looking day by day;
Waiting once again to see
    Blossom dowered, laughing May.
Sunny queen of balmy hours,
    Give again the flowers their hue;
Pearl them with thy glittering showers
    And with coronets of dew.

THE TRUEST NOBLE IN THE LAND.

The truest noble in the land
   Is he who strives to aid the poor;
Then let me proudly grasp his hand,
   And share his joys—I ask no more!
The noblest deeds are those that aim
   To sanctify the people's cause,
To break their wrongs and hide their shame,
   And bind them with the kindest laws!

The truest noble ever born
   Is he who earns the people's thanks,
Who may have won the hate and scorn
   Of fashion's proud and gilded ranks;
But honour crowns the honest heart,
   Whose strength is God-like for the weak,
That fearless acts the hero's part
   And grasps the rights slaves dare not seek!

God gird Thy power, firm as a shield,
    Round him whose voice is loud and long
For human right ; for he may wield
    His thoughts to cancel kingly wrong !
Raise up a noble in each land
    To wrestle for the hungering poor ;
To free the suppliant slaves who stand,
    At king's behest, in chains and gore !

By deeds true nobleness is made,
    And he's the noblest man who dares
Each solemn cause of right to aid
    In words strong as a martyr's prayers ;
And works to see each despot hurled
    Down from the throne his rule profanes,
And in his mind can see the world
    In peace, uncurst by slavery's chains !

SUMMER.

No cloud is in the azure sky,
    The wind with odours laden
The banks of thyme goes fluttering by,
    Light as a graceful maiden.
The young geranium flowers unclose
    And swing in scarlet clusters,
The bee goes humming by the rose
    Where dews make rainbow lustres.

The sun upon the laurel shines,
    Unto the lark we listen,
The woodbine round the hawthorn twines,
    The brooklets sing and glisten.
The merry birds in blossoms hide,
    The poplars faintly quiver,
Their shadows lying side by side
    Across the rippled river.

The blue-bells bloom in trembling ranks,
    The distant meadows shimmer;
On breezy hills and emerald banks
    The golden gorse-flowers glimmer.
All lovely things their charms unfurl
    And wed, for nought is single;
The rarest hues of pink and pearl
    Upon the wild rose mingle.

Oh! what a palace of delight
    Is earth with summer glowing,
We feel each warm and starry night
    The scented south winds blowing.
When dies away the light of stars
    In glimmerings cool and tender,
The east its rosy smile unbars
    To flush old earth with splendour.

And like a lover earth is kissed,
    The sun, her lover, beaming
And sparkling through her veil of mist
    To wake her from her dreaming!
She wears through day's unclouded hours
    Gifts of her lover's wreathing,
The while she proudly shows her flowers
    Her love in perfumes breathing.

FROST ON THE PANES.

The hills are mantled with the snow,
    It lies untrodden in the lanes,
The north winds in sharp chorus blow
    Upon the quaintly frosted panes.
King Frost a rare old artist seems,
    Now on the window trace his skill,
Just as the sun now faintly teems
    His silvery rays adown each hill.

See, on this pane, what magic scenes:
    A palace crowned with many domes,
Such as might charm the proudest queens,
    Transcending all their sumptuous homes.
There stand tall trees, whose leaves look blown
    By sudden tempest all aside;
And birds appear as though they'd flown
    Among the tangled boughs to hide.

And on the pane beside there glows
   An image of a sleeping saint;
What grace about her drapery flows!
   Her lips, how chaste! her cheeks, how faint!
And there a forest rises up;
   There fountains fling on high their spray;
A maiden with a floral cup
   Kneels down 'mong unblown flowers to pray!

Below, the open woods reveal
   Grass wealthy with luxuriant flowers,
While gazing, on the vision steal
   Rare statues, obelisks, and towers!
What mimic grandeur and what grace
   King Frost can pencil on the panes,
While through his work we dimly trace
   The snow-flakes in the fields and lanes!

STAY, DEAR MAIDEN.

Stay, dear maiden, in the dell,
    Stay until the night comes on;
With thy presence there's a spell
    Lost, but loved, when thou art gone.
Soon the moments pass away
    As I linger by thy side;
All my pleasure comes when day
    Down the reddened west has died.

When like bright thought comes the moon,
    Rippling, floating clouds between;
When with dews the roses swoon,
    In my heart thou art a queen.
When the zephyrs faintly blow,
    When the birds have ceased to sing,
When thou whisperest mild and low,
    I am happier than a king.

Haste not from the dell, dear maid,
    Now the white moon floods the skies,
Laurel leaves our forms will shade,
    Shrine each whisper till it dies.
If the stars, love, watch us here,
    All thy beauty they must see;
I 'd not have them, love, too near,—
    They might win thy heart from me.

If the winds thy curls have swayed,
    Made them flutter on thy cheek,
Round them but a moment stayed,—
    'T was thy grace they came to seek.
In the meadow and the dell
    Day and night I own thy powers,
And for time my love to tell
    I would make the moments hours.

AN ELEGY.

No longer happy dreams are mine,
   I see no pleasure now in store;
Lone memories of the lost one twine
    About my heart for evermore,
    Pale fragments of the sweetest lore.

The relics here of her I praised
    Serve only to unlock my tears;
The brightest idol ever raised
    Some tinge of sadness ever wears,
    Weaves sorrow for the coming years.

The heart is made to hold the cares
    It fain would shun from childhood's morn:
The languid look its anguish bares:
    The gayest pleasures ever born
    Some darkened tint of woe have worn.

Ah! could we ne'er recall the past,
  The present would have less of pain:
The shadows on our pathway cast
  Would swiftly as the moments wane,
  And life far happier visions gain.

A look! what histories it reveals,
  What meanings oft start from a word:
The humblest death a life oft seals,
  Whose pangs are never seen or heard,
  Yet nigh to hopeless madness stirred.

Some treasure for the heart we find,
  We place it there as child will lay
A kind fond look upon its mind,
  That hallows it but for a day,
  Then glides in bitter tears away.

The truest hearts are soonest chilled,
  The fairest cheeks the soonest pale;
That life with woe the soonest filled
  Can speak the keenest, saddest tale:
  The rarest joys the soonest fail.

A poor dead idol now I see,
  In memory white and pure it strays;
I ask why was she dear to me?
  She lived in Love's most roseate rays,
  And Love in pensive passion prays.

Rest thou in peace, my lovely one!
    Thy books are records ever dear;
Though like a faded star thou'rt gone,
    I have thy flowers and music here;
    I look to heaven and see thee there!

THE ARTIST.

Tired with the labours of the day,
    And wearied with their cares,
An artist seeks his humble bed—
    Asks God for help in prayers:
Few know the deeds and splendid works
    The man of genius dares.

His mind aspires o'er earthly things
    In quest of high renown,
He only sleeps when woe has crushed
    And bent his spirits down;
While in his dreams he sees the blaze
    Of Fame's immortal crown.

Too oft for him earth's outward things
    Have but a saddened look,
He searches Nature for his theme,
    And reads it as a book;
It buds and blossoms in his mind
    Like violets in a nook.

O radiant genius, thy rare touch
   Is as a magic rod,
Great wonders burst forth from thy skill
   As flowers rise from the sod;
Thou art the power by which we trace
   The majesty of God.

Thou 'rt with the artist in his dreams;
   Thou art a priceless dower;
Thou enterest his toiling mind
   As sunbeams flood a bower;
Thy fancies more enchanting than
   Pink blossoms in a shower.

It may be that from marble block
   A form of grace appears—
Like angel rising from a cloud—
   And praise the artist hears:
The finished figure in his room
   Life-like upon him stares.

Upon the canvas there may rise
   A form to glad the eye,
In lines as though the pencil caught
   Its colours from the sky,
When like a bright exhausted god,
   The sun sinks down to die.

Though want may come, it cannot blind
    His glance at Beauty's shrine,
Nor blast the images that live
    And round his genius shine :
Though tortured with the cares of life
    His labours are divine.

Oh ! great the power given to man,
    To view in humblest things
Great treasures hidden to the mass—
    To soar on Fancy's wings
To where grand Inspiration dawns
    And thought eternal springs.

With sculpture and with painting too—
    They light the darkened mind.
What life may from a statue gleam,
    Though marble-limbed and blind :
For they who look at Nature's heart
    The path to greatness find.

True genius is the lightning spark
    That leaps along the brain,
And they who feel its quickening thrill
    Earn an immortal strain :
The sculptor's and the painter's works
    Through countless centuries reign.

Perchance full on the canvas lives
    The likeness of a maid,
In softest sunshine she may smile,
    'Mong water-lilies wade,
Her curls close by her shoulders blown.
    As though by zephyrs swayed.

Beside a low and rustic stile
    A graceful maiden stands,
And near her lean white-blossomed boughs,
    Not fairer than her hands;
Her glance as bright as crystal drops
    Sunlit on golden sands.

In lowly room, from marble cut,
    A massive figure towers,
Upon the brow a grandeur sits,
    Sign of gigantic powers,
Of one whose labours of the brain
    Each mind with wonder dowers.

And there may stand a beauteous form
    Half naked—bosom bare—
The glance, all bashful, upward turned—
    Hands clasped as though in prayer:
So perfect, that a look of grace
    Pervades her unbound hair.

O thou poor artist! Beauty's slave!
    I venerate thy skill,
Above thy fellow men thou art
    High as the grandest hill:
With poverty thou should'st not meet
    Could I but have my will.

IN SORROW.

The wondrous wheels of life will turn
    When I am seen on earth no more,
The sun as bright in heaven will burn,
    The sea still flap the tawny shore;
The daisies still will snow the sod,
    The vestal snowdrop sweetly spring.
The heavens reflect the power of God,
    The woods with birds' loud warblings ring.
Sad thoughts of that dread time come on;
    What is our doom when life is spent?
Our joys as soon as seen are gone,
    Appear but for one moment sent.
Would I could live as lives the rose,
    Unconscious of a time of gloom,
Or be the humblest flower that grows,
    Forgotten when I ceased to bloom!
This life, so short, so full of fears,
    Has only fitful dreams of rest:
Where are the eyes that shed no tears?
    And where is one unsorrowing breast?

To me the earth seems yet as young
   As when I lived in youth's fair clime,
The sky as bright above me hung,
   The stars as silent and sublime.
But I am changed, and feebler beats
   This heart, where hope is nearly dead;
Each throb the warning but repeats
   That all its best delights are shed.

HER RAVEN CURLS.

Her raven curls on shoulders fall
   Whose whiteness far transcends the snow.
And yet that beauty is not all
   That dwells with her I yearn to know.
What dew is to the summer flower
   Her lustrous glances are to me ;
She dowers me with her witching power,—
   Her form in dreams I only see.

What would I give to be the wind
   That lifts at morn her raven curls ;
What would I give one hour to bind
   Her brow, as white as rarest pearls.
E'en slavery will not leave the land
   While such a maid I daily meet :
I'd give the world to clasp her hand,
   Or kneel a suppliant at her feet.

For light as snow-flakes on the bough
    She trips the flowering meadows o'er,
While I have breathed an ardent vow
    To win her love—or love no more.
Within my heart, as in a shrine,
    Her image dwells all bright and rare,
And were the proudest empire mine
    I'd have no joy she should not share.

LADY GERTRUDE.

Lady Gertrude is a young brunette
   With a pair of dazzling eyes
Whose likeness in stars is only met
   When the moon begins to rise.
Lady Gertrude has two clusters of curls
   Whose hue is a lustrous brown,
And, sprung from a line of wealthy earls,
   Has a brow to grace a crown!

Lady Gertrude in the garden strays
   And walks by the placid lake,
And sees it kissed by the morning's rays
   When green leaves over it shake.
Lady Gertrude has a fair white hand,
   Her cheek has a wild-rose hue,
Lightly she'll kiss the lilies that stand
   In a morning dream of dew!

Lady Gertrude has no haughty pride,
   Her voice has a silvery tone;
What would I give to call her my bride,
   And she to call me her own!
Violets hidden in dew-laden dell
   So shy did never appear,
A footstep lighter never yet fell
   On a listening lover's ear!

Lady Gertrude never heeds my looks,
   I worship her but in vain;
Were I but one of her treasured books
   What pleasure then I could gain!
Lady Gertrude with her harp in the morn
   In a vine-bower plays and sings,
The sun, though it fails her form to adorn,
   Will toy with her jewelled rings!

Lady Gertrude is the dearest to me
   In summer and autumn eves,
With her in the twilight I would be
   By the whispering laurel leaves.
Lady Gertrude has a nameless grace
   And music in every speech,
Beauty and love in her looks I trace,
   And see that she's queen of each!

OUR TOILERS.

Our toilers earth's proud kingdoms grace,
    They rear the glory of a land
Where Labour's skill and might we trace,
    The wealthiest, proudest nobles stand.
The subtle labours of the mind
    Give splendours to each nation's name;
That country blessed with art will find
    The brightest, broadest path to fame.

Our toilers pile our golden stores,
    Are brawny giants of the State,
The sturdy bulwarks of our shores,
    Men who have made Old England great.
They bear their daily burdens well,
    And guard our throne with iron will,
While other lands their valour tell,
    Awed with the wonders of their skill.

Our toilers are the men who build
    Old England's grandeur far and wide ;
The mighty strokes of Labour gild
    Her seas and shores, her wishes guide.
Our toilers strike each burning spark
    From Labour's heart to set like gold,
And from earth's caverns cold and dark
    Our riches and our treasures mould.

Stern Labour carves a nation's power,
    With Time it wrestles like a god,
Stands up majestic as a tower,
    Surveys the skies or ploughs the sod.
And everywhere its strength is seen,
    Aloud its strong great pulses beat ;
Plains change to glory where it 's been,
    And nations through its prowess meet.

THE MISER AND HIS GOLD.

Dark was the night, the raindrops beat
    And cracked on the window panes,
While the winds went howling down the street
    And roared in the village lanes;
The black clouds hung like funeral palls
    Over the meadows and plains.

Not a star was seen to deck the sky,
    Not an azure rent was seen,
But all above was black as the face
    Of an Oriental queen:
Not a sign was left to tell how bright
    The beautiful day had been.

The leafless boughs of the giant trees
    Rattled like skeleton's bones,
The restless winds in the gardens moaned
    Like a host of wrinkled crones;
The pitiless rain in a turgid stream,
    Rushed madly over the stones.

A miser sate in his darkened room—
    Chilly and damp was the air;
He crouched upon the carpetless floor,
    Like a panther in his lair;
He listened and thought he heard a foot
    Slowly ascending the stair.

A sickening thrill leapt through his frame,
    And his hands grew pale and cold,
And quicker than lightning sped a thought
    That a felon sought his gold :
In the rag that hung on his wasted form
    His meagre body he rolled.

The walls of his room were dark and bare,
    The windows were dim with dust,
No firelight flashed in the dismal grate,
    The bars were covered with rust;
For the miser pined for heaps of gold
    With a never-ending lust.

If sunbeams entered his room by day,
    'Mid squalor they seemed to faint,
They made the miser's countenance wan,
    Like harlot's cheek robbed of paint :
His stony heart, like his ghastly face
    Was blurred with a moral taint.

He hated the genial light of day
   As it lay on his wretched bed ;
His brow was dry as an autumn leaf,
   And his eyes sunk deep in his head :
Such eyes ! that ne'er showed feeling and fire,
   But cold and icy as lead !

For guilty thoughts ran over his mind,
   As lurid as burning coals,
While anguish struck through his withered
      frame
   Like the pains in murderers' souls,
The last few moments before they meet
   Their dreaded eternal goals.

His shrivelled hands with a tremor shook
   And beat on the dusty floor ;
The gold he had was dearer to him
   Than all a philosopher's lore ;
His blood surged colder unto his heart
   Than e'er it had done before.

A thought of a deed in years gone by
   Filled his mind with perilous dread ;
Through the darkness on the floor he saw
   Blood-drops gleam freshly and red—
The blood of one he 'd secretly slain,
   Like a curse before him spread.

He had lured a friend into his room,
    To whom he prated of gold,
One winter night when the earth was white,
    Wrapped deep in a snowy fold :
And long were the tales of hoarded wealth
    That miserable miser told.

They talked till the midnight hour drew near.
    And the hideous miser planned
A scheme of murder, and struck his friend
    With a knife clasped in his hand ;
And the hot blood spurted from his breast.
    And smoked like a burning brand !

The watchful stars had sprinkled the sky,—
    Through the window peered like eyes,
While the miser's face grew hot and red ;
    And deep were the dying sighs
Of the bleeding victim at his feet,
    Whose presence he 'd won with lies.

He shook when he felt the gory corpse,
    And a chill crept like a snake,
Clammy and cold, to his iron heart
    When he bent its gold to take :
A pain shot through his shivering frame,
    Like culprit pierced with a stake.

In a secret part of his filthy home
    The plundered corpse he laid,
And covered it o'er with rags and stones
    Until the flesh was decayed,
Then broke the bones and buried them deep
    In a secret grave he'd made.

Years glided on, and he ever saw
    The ghost of his murdered guest—
For ever he saw him by his side,
    The gory gash in his breast:
The miser's sleep was broken by groans,
    Like a murderer's last night's rest!

He thought he heard a foot on the stair,
    At the door a gentle tap,
And the wrinkles round his evil eyes
    Were like the lines on a map,
While a figure slid into the room
    In a whitened shroud and cap.

The deepest darkness shadowed the room,
    And the miser dared not speak,
Each hurrying moment seemed an hour,
    Each hour as long as a week,
And as the ghostly figure walked forth
    The old floor began to creak!

But faintly the miser dared to breathe,
    And his face grew damp and wan,
Like torrents of lava through his veins
    The vile blood bubbled and ran.
Oh! great was the terror and dismay
    Of that old gold-loving man!

Slowly the ghostly figure moved on,
    With a calm step to and fro,
While before the miser's anxious eyes
    Young demons stood in a row—
Large azure sparks from their fingers dropt,
    And fire-rings circled each brow.

A moment they stood, then disappeared;
    Like statue the figure stood;
In his hand was clasped a club like Cain's,
    Of black and heaviest wood:
The miser believed he saw it dashed
    And spattered with drops of blood.

Now, suddenly, in that cheerless room
    Shone a light most faint and thin,
The miser beheld not where it grew,
    Nor how it came gliding in;
With a blistering force it seemed to scorch
    His filthy and wrinkled skin.

His tongue seemed palsied between his lips,
   His heart throbbed loud in his breast,
As ponderous as an iron ball,
   And broke his chances of rest ;
A host of horrors dwelt on his brain,
   Red phantoms around him prest !

Quick as when lightning strikes the eye
   Grim goblins about him stood,
And capered awhile, then slid away,
   Each head bound up with a hood
Of the whitest texture, stained around
   With fading blotches of blood.

Their limbs were wrapped in a darkened garb,
   And a skeleton each one held :
When the miser saw their eyeless skulls
   The ghastliest terrors swelled
In torturing troops upon his soul,
   Too raging to be quelled.

The figure glared with its bloodshot eyes—
   Half-blinded the miser's look,
Who thought upon the innocent life,
   For gold, he once basely took ;
A blood-spot stood before his gaze
   Like a huge lie in a book !

" Where are the bones," the figure cried out,
" Of that poor and murdered man,
Whose guiltless blood on thy filthy floor
   In a smoking torrent ran ?
Now justify that cardinal crime
   Against your God, if you can."

The miser trembled, and not a word
   Crept forth from his stiffened tongue,
When the figure cried, " Unto the damned
   Of the earth thou dost belong :"
In the miser's ears young demons sang
   A wild and baleful song.

And then from the figure's garments crawled
   A hissing and hungry snake,
And upon the miser straight it sprang,—
   Pierced his body like a stake :
He yelled and fell—no more on the earth
   To murder or to wake.

The figure then vanished, and the snake ;
   On the floor the miser lay ;
And full on his cold and rigid corpse
   Streamed forth the light of next day :
And yet in that room may still be seen
   His bones half mouldered away.

A DREAM OF THE FAIRIES.

At eve, when wearied with my toil,
    I sat in quiet in my chair,
And through the open window came
    In cooling waves the evening air,
With fragrance laden from the flowers,
    That under opened blossoms swung,
And where, like gleaming bowers of gold,
    Laburnum flowers in sunshine hung.

Sleep came upon me, and a dream,
    With fairies thronged, upon me grew;
And unto each the laughing queen
    Full-blown and dew-drenched roses threw.
While round my chair they danced about,
    And with the odorous roses played,
I thought I saw an ivory bowl
    Upon a bank of blue-bells laid.

The bowl was filled with sparkling dew,
    From which each merry fairy sipped;
Like rills their tiny laughter flowed—
    The tripping wantons—cherry lipped!
Young twittering birds around me flew,
    The fairies gambolled at my feet;
I saw their little silver wings,
    Like closing leaves of lilies, meet.

The sportive elves around me came,
    And flung their roses in my face;
And then they ran 'mong purple vines,
    The amber-plumaged birds to chase.
They frisked about my knee and smiled,
    And then they whispered in my ears;
I felt I could not sleep when teazed
    With such a pretty host of dears.

Around the roses still they flung
    And, laughing, waved their silver wands,
Then sang a strain I faintly heard,
    "We fly, we fly to flowery lands."
And next among the blue-bells hid—
    A moment only lost to view—
Then hand in hand they danced around
    The ivory bowl of sparkling dew.

I woke ; that dream was like the thoughts
    That charm us when the heart is young :
When cloudless love and roses make
    The dearest pleasures seen or sung !

A FRAGMENT.

I believe in all that is good in man,
    In every creed,
That helps to form and mould a nobler plan,
    From errors freed.
I honour the rich and pity the proud
    In every sphere;
Whenever I gaze on the toiling crowd
    My heart is there.

I know the struggles of the helpless poor,
    For I have felt
That gifts to them from pleasure's radiant store
    Are feebly dealt.
And therefore I rejoice when men of power
    Their efforts give
Unto the people as a precious dower
    That they may live.

In darksome alleys where the toilers pine
    Should Love be heard ;
There should Hope's bow of beauty ever shine,
    Joy speak a word.
To help a brother is my duty first,
    To soothe his soul
Ere deepest sorrows o'er him darkly burst
    And hot tears roll.

The solemn histories of the hungered mass,
    Pens dipped in fire
Could never write ; to graves they pass,
    Poor maid and sire,
Unwept, unknown, save by the lonely few
    They leave behind ;
To whom the world has not one hopeful view
    To charm the mind.

Strange that in this vast hive where wealth abounds
    Distress should reign,
Homes ever ring with hoarse and hollow sounds
    From heart and brain !
Yet so it is ; then, nobles, lend a hand
    In causes just ;
Like these poor branded brethren in the land,
    Ye are but dust !

The shriek of madness and the brutal jeer
    Would grow more faint
If mercy lent betimes a willing ear—
    Walked like a saint
To where pale misery, like a wrinkled ghost,
    Unsmiling dwells,
The haggard guest of poverty's lean host,
    Deaf with death-knells !

God placed his watchfires in the gleaming sky
    For man's delight,
And each poor Labourer should flourish by
    His skill and might.
The poor one should not ever work in vain,
    Low as the sod ;
Have faith, poor slaves ! and ye shall one day [gain
    The help of God !

IN THE VILLAGE LANE.

Our home stands in the village lane,
   Where Spring's first blossoms blow,
And where the sunsets slowly wane
   And spend their purple glow.
Where night is still, and not a breeze
   Is heard to stir the flowers,
Nor sway the leaves upon the trees,
   I spend the happiest hours.

I love the air when calm and cool,
   And skies when they are blue,
When water-lilies on the pool
   Lie pearled with morning dew.
About our home the ivy grows,
   There lover-like it dwells;
Around a wavering shadow throws
   When winds come from the dells.

I watch the moon rise pale as saint
    Above the plume-like firs;
I feel the wild-briar odours faint
    When not one leaflet stirs.
The moon's light floods the affluent skies,
    Swims through the palaced clouds;
The murmur of a fountain dies,
    Stars pant in wealthy crowds.

And when the Summer mornings wake
    My chamber windows shine
Like ripples sun-fired on a lake,
    While slowly moves the vine.
I hear the wild birds loudly sing
    Where daintiest blossoms blow,
And through the vales their warblings ring
    Where moss-banked brooklets flow.

And when the orchard trees are crowned
    With bloom, rare sweets are born—
The faintest odours, and dew-drowned,
    Wild roses blush at morn,
As though afraid to show their leaves
    With dew-drops gemmed and hushed,
And being kissed by summer eves,
    They met the morn and blushed!

THE BIRD IS SINGING IN THE TREE.

The bird is singing in the tree,
   Lightly falls the cooling shower;
But, maid, I am no longer free,
   I am captive by thy power.
I would be free as yonder bird,
   Fluttering where the lilies are,
And listen to each warbled word
   Linked to tones of thy guitar.

Thy cheeks like apple blossoms glow,
   Dainty charms I yearn to reach;
Oh! pouting lips, what raptures flow—
   Lips that lend a charm to speech!
Say, why should words of thine be spells,
   Fetters to enchant and bind?
By night and day thy witchery dwells
   Dear as treasure on the mind.

Didst thou but know my heart was thine
    Unto me thy own might turn ;
Sweetest hopes of thee are mine,
    Hopes that with love's lustres burn.
By day and night I live the same,
    Wishing for thy heart and hand ;
For fairer form and fairer name
    Never, never graced the land.

Thine eyes, what bright alluring deeps!
    Spell-like orbs that lure me on ;
Thy form in midnight slumber keeps
    Standing near me, worshipped one !
Hearts must have idols while they live,
    Gladdening well this world of ours ;
To thee my heart I fondly give,
    Oh ! sweeter than the spring-time flowers !

KATE.

Lovely the light of Autumn hours,
    Lovely to walk with thee, dear Kate;
And lovely the blushes of the flowers—
    Lilac bloom at the garden gate;
And lovely to wander down the lane,
    Watching the sun in crimson swoon;
Watching the upland and the plain,
    Argently gleam in the rising moon.

Lovely to listen to thy words
    When zephyrs the myrtles pass by;
When the evening has hushed the birds,
    And dissolved in a violet sky!
And happier far thy look to me
    Than the meadow, valley, or stream;
Heedless of care when clasping thee,
    Entranced of the future I dream.

Lovely when morning's purple hues
    From the hills and the valleys fade;
Lovely to see how rich with dews
    By night have the meadows been made.
I list thee, Kate, where laurels flower,
    And proud to thy presence I haste;
Briefer than moment passes each hour
    When fondly I 'm clasping thy waist.

LADY ALICE.

In the sunshine in the garden
    I and Lady Alice met,
When the bloom upon the peaches
    Like a maiden's blush had set.
In a cool bower roofed with laurel
    Oft would Lady Alice dwell,
In the waning of the evening,
    Toying with a silver bell.

On a couch of richest velvet
    Still as statue she 'd recline,
Reading lovely-worded poems,
    Lingering on each glowing line.
Through her bower the rose's odours
    Floated on the zephyr's wings,
And the sunshine kissed the diamonds
    Set like dewdrops in her rings.

I have envied oft the moonlight
    As I 've seen it braid her hair,
Yet it lost its own pale beauty
    When it touched a form so fair.
I was proud that daintiest violet
    Had no tint to match her eye,
That its likeness only sparkled
    In a warm and azure sky.

She 'd a mind of rarest beauty,
    Like a leaf as gently swayed,
Sweet as moon that looks from heaven
    On the brightness it has made.
In the sunshine in the garden,
    Or in her laurelled bower,
Live my thoughts with Lady Alice
    As the perfumes with a flower.

IN THE AUTUMN OF THE YEAR.

Slowly rising o'er the woodland
   I beheld the moon appear,
Like a pale and naked maiden
   In the Autumn of the year.
In the blue sky meekly palaced,
   Up the clouds it seemed to swim;
And the light poured like a river
   From its white and lustrous rim.

And the lake had not a ripple
   Where the moon's rich image sank;
While its glory from the heavens
   Glittered down the blue bell bank.
'Round her orb the stars were trembling
   Like a swarm of golden gems,
Till the queenly moon looked wealthy,
   With her burning diadems.

In the calm deep hush of Autumn,
    When the fruits hang round and ripe,
When like golden orbs the apples
    Show a faint and crimson stripe—
Then I feel a touch of gladness
    Playing round my heart and brain,
And I listen to the whispers
    Of the wind among the grain;

For old Autumn is the artist
    Whose delicious beauty tips
Fading leaves with hues of ruby,
    Fresh as glow of ruddy lips.
And its hues of dainty amber
    Tint the hedges in the lane,
When the sun sinks, flushed and vanquished.
    In his warm red splendour slain.

On the past I'm led to wonder
    As I muse at eve alone;
When I view in Autumn evenings
    Faded leaves from musk-rose blown:
Like the hopes that fall for ever,
    Bearing joys too quickly o'er;
As a wave the moonlight tramples,
    Glimmers once, but gleams no more.

THE NIGHT BEFORE THE WEDDING MORN.

The night before the wedding morn
   With round cheeks flushed the maiden lies;
The veins about her temples seem
   Like sapphire gleam of summer skies.
One arm was curved with such a grace
   That art of sculptor could not reach;
The faintest hue of pink it bore,
   Like snow-wreath tinged with blooming peach.

Upon the pillow lay her curls,
   On either side a raven crowd.
I ne'er before had seen a maid
   So beauty-dowered, so whitely browed;
Her shoulders, fair as whitest rose,
   Were warm and full, and running round
Her brow a coronet was seen
   In midnight's mingled beauty drowned.

A scarlet flush was on her lips,
   That oped betimes, then gently stirred
As though the maiden sought to speak
   In balmy whisper one sweet word.
Full blown carnations never shed
   Such sweets as from those young lips
      flowed ;
Such tresses never drooped before
   In such a large and lustrous load.

She lay hushed in the sunny morn,
   Whose silvery luxuries cast pale charms
About her face and on her hair,
   While naked lay her unclasped arms ;
Calm as a statue long she dreamed ;
   Her left hand, light and graceful, prest
The model of a dove in gold,
   Couched on her ivory-tinted breast.

TO THE MOON.

Like maiden pale and wan with fear
   Thou swimmest up the murky night;
A star below thee, like a tear,
   Throbs in thy cool and snowy light.
Like swimmer gliding to the shore
   I see thee climb night's spangled roof;
I would that I could with thee soar,
   Swathed in thy beams of silver woof.

The starry night seems proud of thee,
   My sad gaze measures thy domain;
The stars around thee unto me
   Stand out like drops of golden rain.
I watch the clouds about thee sail
   As banks of snow to make thee dim,
While o'er their summits sadly pale
   Shines forth thy white and pearly rim!

Oh ! voiceless virgin ! Maid of Night !
   The sapphire sky's pellucid crown !
I revel in thy vestal light
   Whose rays the hills in splendours drown.
Thou calm, unlanguaged goddess glow !
   Oft with thy praise the lyre has rung,
Thou 'st seen uncounted centuries flow,
   And still thou 'rt beautiful and young.

I love to see thee gild the skies,
   Dissolving night's grand ebon gloom ;
Old ocean in thy glory lies,
   Sleeps in thy white eternal bloom !
Thy smiles on tree and flower I trace,
   I meet them on the vernal sod ;
Thou type of patience and of grace,
   The dumb great midnight's crest of God !

THE STATUES.

A PALACE door I entered and I saw
   In marble formed a naked maiden stand;
Her silent beauty filled my soul with awe,
   She held a lily in her right white hand.
Through windows stained with violet and gold
   The light was flattered to her rounded face;
It kissed her neck, whose rare and ample mould
   Seemed the abode of Art's transcendent grace.
The poppies at her feet had leaves half shut
In cold, luxuriant clusters carved and cut!

Back from her brow her hair seemed lightly
   blown
   And down her shoulders in curled masses
      fell;
Large signs of life unto her eyes had flown
   Like those that on a sleeper's eyelids dwell.

A nameless grace had made her polished look
    Appear half conscious of her unclad limbs,
And from her bosom oft my glance I took
    As from a wave that dazzles as it swims.
The soul of Genius in that figure taught
The sterling wealth and wonder of a thought!

Hard by another sculptured form I met,
    'Twas of a hero with deep furrowed cheek
That told of labour; and his lips were set
    As though unto the gazer he would speak.
One hand was clenched, and swelled the rigid veins,
    Gorged as with burning blood his stalwart arm,—
As though he strove to wrench a captive's chains,
    Or fiercely struggled for some wrested charm;
A tragic meaning in his glance long dared
As if on some old hated foe he stared!

His hard and wrinkled brow was deep and wide,
    No trace of smile upon the features played;
Unawed by death he would have firmly died
    With deep gashed heart cut by a foeman's blade.

A few stray curls around his shoulders hung,
    But time had left his massive temples bare ;
Upon his face the sign of age had flung ;
    His iron frame bent with a weight of care ;
While from his stony eyeballs strong and stern,
Like fire unslaked proud passion seemed to
        burn !

WISHES.

Oh! would I were the bird that pours
   His song into thine ear,
I would not sigh for sunny shores
   While thou, my love, wast near.
Oh! could I choose my heaven on earth,
   I 'd whisper it to thee;
'T would be all other pleasures worth—
   An Eden unto me!

If I were but the jewelled band
   Of gold around thy arm,
I 'd glide betimes unto thy hand,
   And clasp it as a charm.
I 'd be the poems thou dost read
   In summer evenings dim,
That I might all the glories heed
   That in thy dark eyes swim.

I 'd be the mirror where by morn
    Thou lookest in so sweet,
To hold each smile when newly born,
    Then watch thy red lips meet.
I 'd be a zephyr but one hour
    To wanton on thy cheek,
To shake thy ringlets in a shower,
    And list to hear thee speak.

The gem that glimmers on thy breast
    I 'd be, for I should shine
With rarer beauty from such rest
    By winning charms from thine.
Each thing thou ownest I would be,
    And feel thy warm caress ;
By day a dove embraced by thee,
    By night a raven tress !

THE DEAD ONE'S GRAVE.

Now pause awhile, for here's the grave
    Of one who ever loved us well,
As fair and good as she was brave—
    But poor this pen her worth to tell.
Above her grave the low wind sweeps
    Like mourner's sigh, while in our hearts
Her form its place of fondness keeps,
    And sometimes on our vision starts.

Now all is darkness where she strayed,
    The pleasure once we felt is gone,
In secret for her soul we've prayed—
    Our loveliest and our dearest one.
With pale white hand she touched the flowers,
    And now they for her fondness pine;
We see her yet in midnight hours,
    All saintly in a marble shrine.

This stone above her grave records
   Not half the virtues of her mind ;
The purest and the sweetest words
   For her dear name the living find.
The timid blush upon each cheek
   Seemed there by loving angels placed :
We thought that could the flowerets speak
   They 'd own her look their beauty graced.

Upon some spot we linger long,
   Once graced by one who lives no more,
As when we 're charmed by some sad song
   When all its melody is o'er.
And by this grave we meet to rest,
   To shed the tears that grief has made :
For hearts by sorrow daily prest
   Cling where their poor dead treasure 's laid.

TO AURORA.

Aurora, gentle goddess! did
  Orion clasp thy waist
When first upon thy shining form
  His ardent glance he placed?
Say, were thy curls with dews besprent,
  And were thy feet sun-bound?
Did golden clouds thy radiant breast
  Float lovingly around?

And did Hyperion see thee eye
  Orion in the chase,
Thou sun-browed goddess of the morn
  With dew-besprinkled face?
Where didst thou gain thy rosy hues?
  And was Tithonus thine?
When on Cephalus did thy look
  Of bliss begin to shine?

Did Hesperus watch thy amours
   Ere Jupiter was born—
Ere Venus through Adonis set
   Her foot upon the thorn?
Was Saturn envious of thy love?
   Did Pallas gaze on thee?
Hast watched thy own rare beauties throw
   Red glimmers on the sea?

Did Titan envy thee thy power?
   Did Procris learn thy skill?
Didst gaze on bound Prometheus on
   The cold Caucasian hill?
Didst gaze on the Hesperian fruits
   Ere wise Deucalion stood
On Mount Parnassus—ere was spilt
   In war the Titan's blood?

IN YONDER COT.

In yonder cot a maiden lives,
   A simple maiden I adore;
And there the morning sunshine gives
   A kiss to ivy round the door.
I see this cottage in the morn,
   Where dwells my poor but graceful maid;
And wish I'd been a sunbeam born,
   Within her deep blue eyes to wade.

Plain is her beauty, yet it bears
   A charm no words could ever paint;
The bloom upon each cheek appears
   As though 't were borrowed from a saint.
And when the bees hum 'mong the flowers,
   And each its draught of honey sips,
I'd gladly pass the fleeting hours
   In stealing glances of her lips.

Art has no power to make her vain;
   There Nature's gifts are only seen;
Each spot a brightness seems to gain,
   Where she has but a moment been.
Beyond the cottage where she dwells
   The old church rears its ancient spire;
And to that church when chime the bells
   The maiden walks beside her sire!

I follow with a beating heart
   Through flowering fields and rustic lanes,
When down the air in ripples start
   The sun-winged skylark's trembling strains;
My glance will wander to her own
   As in the church I hear her sing;
I 've said I 'll make my passion known,
   And one day slowly name the ring!

THE CASTLE BY THE RHINE.

A KING dwelt in a castle
　　Close by the limpid Rhine,
And red his face with lipping
　　Of mellow flushing wine.
Gloom on his brow was ever,
　　By day and night 'twas seen;
His face was scarred with wrinkles,
　　And cold as corpse I ween.

When died away the daylight,
　　His heart with fear was wild;
In strength he was a giant,
　　In bravery a child.
Against the castle windows
　　The swinging ivy beat,
Like sound of demons' fingers—
　　The demons he must meet.

None dared to reach the castle,
 " 'T is haunted," people cried ;
The king, they said, had murdered
 His beautiful young bride.
The king by night would shiver
 Like banner from a tower ;
A ghost before him fluttered
 At every midnight hour.

In phial he had treasured
 Drops of his victim's blood ;
The oaken floor was spattered,
 And deluged in a flood.
Years passed, and there it lingered,
 No work removed the stains ;
At midnight groaned the murderer,
 Like black slave in his chains.

When sleeping hosts of demons
 He saw in frightful dreams,
And flames that curled like serpents
 Wriggled in reddened streams.
His slumber had no soundness,
 He knew not balmy rest,
And guilt of wondrous greatness
 Lay gnawing at his breast.

One dark and dreary midnight
   He groped about for wine,
And clutched the bloody phial—
   By moonlight saw it shine.
Hot in his thirst and agony
   He knew not what he drank;
He quaffed the blood and staggered,
   Then stiff and lifeless sank.

'T is many, many years ago,
   And still the castle stands,
The floor yet stained with blood-drops
   Spilt by the murderer's hands.
And since no one has entered,
   No one the castle owns;
There may be seen, yet bleaching,
   The murderer's fleshless bones!

THE POETRY OF EARTH.

Old earth in vernal beauty lies,
    The trees bow to the flowers,
A mellow glory floods the skies,
    The grass is bathed with showers.
A calm sweet spirit walks the air,
    Each leaf and blossom thrills;
This ruddy morn all things are fair,
    From sky to plashing rills.

The banks are sunlit, and the moss
    Is cool with glittering dews,
Wild hyacinths the low winds toss,
    Clouds part with azure views.
The odours from the new mown hay
    Run through each leafy bush,
The violets from each woodland way
    Send up a purple blush.

Of wealthy blooms all redly rimmed
    Earth's spirit never tires,
In tears her smile is never dimmed,
    Seas welter in her fires.
Fresh murmurs ripple through the dell,
    Fresh wild flowers hide our feet,
The buds with ripening beauty swell,
    The winds and blossoms meet.

A haze of mellowed glory tips
    All things in summer eves,
The dying sun's red beams, like lips,
    Kiss o'er the dewy leaves.
Swarm up the honeyed sighs of flowers
    Through slowly rising mist,
And, sprinkled with luxuriant showers,
    Each flower yearns to be kist.

ADA.

My Ada, darling, thou art dearest,
   Loveliest creature ever known,
And thy brow is far the fairest—
   All my blessings thou dost own.
In the morning, lightly singing,
   She comes bounding to my knee;
Her little curls in sunlight swinging
   Shower their splendours over me.

I am proud to hear her warble,
   For I'm led from earthly cares;
Pale as saint in polished marble
   As she lisps her evening prayers.
And I watch her mingled graces
   As she runs around my chair,
Till I'm held in soft embraces,
   Touched by feelings light as air.

Knowledge springs from ways most simple,
    Truest when the heart is young,
When the fresh smile wears a dimple,
    Ere the heart with woe is wrung.
Ada, darling, is my lover,
    Through her deeds no stain is seen,
Angels ever round her hover,
    And her wishes heavenward lean.

Night and morn her love revealing,
    I am led by unseen hands,
Heart o'erfilled with tender feeling,
    Where the guardian angel stands!
In dreams by night this child is pouring
    Words like songs into my ears,
Fresh as bird's towards Heaven soaring,
    While I walk divinest spheres.

Each fond word she utters teaches
    Charms I never knew before;
There's a power in childish speeches
    Makes me listen and adore.
May she not too early perish,
    Life so sweet should long remain;
Angels long her glory cherish,
    May her sweetness never wane!

Few the charms that dawn to cheer me.
    Yet this darling child has made
Gleams of holiest pleasure near me.
    Pale dreams on my fancy laid.
For to me this childish maiden
    Brings divinest beauties near;
And my soul with joy is laden
    Till a Heaven surrounds me here!

THE OLD WHEEL IN THE MILL.

In the silence of the evening,
    When the sun has gone to rest,
And left its rosiest glory
    On the river's tranquil breast,
O'er the crumbling bridge I wander,
    Spanning low the limpid rill,
And I listen to the turning
    Of the old wheel in the mill.

Then I watch the water bubble,
    See it struggle from the arch
Of the old mill quaint and mouldering,
    Watch the waves in circles march.
And those waves seem but the symbols
    Of man's labours day by day;
That their power is lost as quickly,
    That they pass as soon away!

On that bridge I pause and wonder
    How poor human nature fares;
How it toils sublime in sorrow,
    And what noble deeds it dares.
How it works and bravely suffers,
    With a never-flagging will,
Like the waves that gush and struggle
    From the old arch of the mill.

When the old mill wheel is silent,
    I am linked unto the scene,
Not a wrinkle scars the water
    O'er whose breast Night's jewels lean.
And the blue sky filled with beauty,
    On the rill a lustre throws,
While the pale moon through the cloudlets
    Opens softly as a rose!

And those moments are the treasures
    Given by the hand of Time,
Teaching us that 'mid our troubles
    Pictures dawn of the sublime,
And that life has woes and sorrows,
    Only sent to fill the mind
With unworded love and reverence
    For the peace we sometimes find!

TO JUNE.

Month of roses! come again,
Month whose smiles the flowerets stain;
In the valley, on the hill,
By the lightly rushing rill;
'Mong the clover and wild briar,
Dewdrops throw like gems of fire!

Month of beauty! come once more,
'Tween green leaves thy sunshine pour;
Cowslips now have left the wold,—
Floral trumpets tipped with gold;
Ope the rosebuds on the bush,
Down where babbling brooklets gush!

Month of splendour! gild the plain,
Fling thy radiance down the lane;
Let thy zephyrs in the dells
Lightly ring the young blue-bells,
Every morn their petals toss
On the banks of thyme and moss!

Month of pleasure! and blue skies,
Let us feel thy southern sighs;
Lustrous artist of the flowers,
Fairy weaver of bright hours;
Beauty's goddess! come again,
Meadows sprinkle with thy rain!

FIRESIDE MUSINGS.

Beside the fire I muse at eve,
    When daily toil is o'er;
Then memory glides unto the past—
    To days that live no more,—
Recounts the pleasure and the joys
    Their happy moments bore.

The scenes have faded one by one,
    Lie buried in the past;
Years are the graves wherein they lie.
    Their shadows only last
Like figure of a tree at eve
    On plain and upland cast.

When mornings came in purple mist.
    And loudly sang the lark
Above the giant oaks that graced
    The wide and level park,
I watched the mild Hesperian star
    Gleam like a diamond spark!

I loved the winds that rocked the wood
   And swept the flowery dell;
The sounds of torrents as they rose,
   Into one mighty swell,—
Like many voices in a crowd,
   That blend their wrongs to tell!

Now as I muse alone there comes
   A form unto my side
That cheered me daily while it lived,
   Smiled on me when it died;
Whose love shone mildly o'er my life,
   Like full moon o'er a tide!

I long to hear its voice again,
   To place its hand in mine;
To gaze into its placid eyes—
   Again behold them shine
With sparkle that appeared akin
   To what must be divine!

I whisper to the form that comes
   Of blessings long since dead,
The happy dreams its loving words
   Through eve and midnight shed,—
The grand delights and sunny views
   To which its glances led.

We walked up hills in setting eves,
    When winds were soft and low,
And all the west with amber beams,
    And purple, seemed to glow;
In which like icebergs flushed with fire
    The broad clouds seemed to flow!

We sought by night the village lane,
    Where lonely wild-flowers swung;
When zephyrs round the blossoms played
    Where birds at morn had sung,
And where the drops of morning dew
    Like bridal gems had hung!

My life was crowned with wedded love,
    But few the treasured years;
That life the soonest leaves the earth
    That most of promise bears;
It weaves the fairest, purest joys,
    Or draws the saddest tears.

For ever as I sit alone
    The form long dead I seek;
I cannot reach its pale cold brow
    Or touch its round white cheek;
It flits before me if I move
    Or form my lips to speak!

In secret oft a solace dawns
    To ease the heart of pain ;
We may behold an idol lost
    Back with us once again,—
We may not with a reverent heart
    Muse with the dead in vain !

UNDER THE HOLLY.

Under the holly at Christmas time
    How gaily the moments pass ;
Upon the trees the ermine rime
    Sparkles in a mass.
    The fire merrily burns
    On the polished urns,
Ruddily gleams the wine in the glass !

While King Frost is bronzing the panes
    His fairy-like works we trace ;
The hedges in the village lanes
    Twinkle with his grace !
    On gossamer lines
    How his pearl-work shines,
When winds in treble chorus race.

Now circling at the festive board
    Friends appear we love to greet ;
We see the ripened wine outpoured,
    Hearts all warmly beat.
    Jovial tales are told
    Of the days of old,
When brightest eyes and faces meet !

Warm on the walls the firelight shines,
    Throws a mellow tint around ;
Gilding the home where friendship twines,
    Then comes forth a sound
    Of joy and of mirth,
    The sweetest on earth,
Where beauty and pleasure are found !

LINES FOR THE POOR.

I 'D gladden the hearts of all the poor
    In every land ;
The wail of sorrow should rise no more
    From that great band.
The tumult of tongues and every strife
    I 'd gladly calm ;
And peace should hallow each toiler's life,
    Sweet as a psalm.

Ever pale discord shatters the springs
    Of love and peace ;
When will this age that with madness rings
    Die out and cease ?
When will shine out a lovelier day
    For bondaged men ?
And all the earth's tyrants pass away,
    Despair cries—when ?

Had I the power to take the earth
    Unto my heart
I 'd ease its sorrow, and labour's worth
    In songs should start.
With a loving hand I 'd dry the tears
    That ever drown
Its beauty; like unto Christ it wears
    A thorny crown.

In alleys and courts gaunt misery stands
    Up like a ghost
Here, in this the noblest of all lands,
    And ruler's boast.
And want never leaves unnumbered homes
    In this proud isle;
There poverty haggard and wrinkled roams
    With hideous smile.

When will the magic of kindness reach
    The hearts of Courts?
Against whose follies the prelates preach,
    And costly sports.
Speak, prelates, to Nature where it pines
    With blinded eyes:
Methinks I see that in the future shines
    Its hour to rise!

LOVE LYRIC.

Come near, my love, this melting eve
    Reminds me of the days no more;
It tells me where my thoughts have been,
    Pale fragments of forgotten lore.
Dost hear the birds sing far and near,
    And see the sun go down the west?
While from each blossom hangs a tear,
    Like opals on a virgin's breast!

Come by the window sit, my love,
    The perfumed breeze will fan thy face,
Yon myrtle tree that heavens a dove
    Will shield from eyes thy sovereign grace.
And we will talk of days gone by,
    In summer when we loved to meet,
When clouds were palaced in the sky,
    Not whiter than thy tiny feet.

All earth was heaven to me, and long
    We roamed 'mong trees whose vernal shades
Lent to the accents of thy tongue
    A sacred charm, my queen of maids.
To thee sighs came from clover flowers,
    The air thy ringlets rippled round
Thy shoulders in rare glossy showers,
    Like marble half in darkness bound.

To me thou wast all that I sought,
    With pride untold I worshipped thee;
What language is to noble thought
    Thy magic beauty was to me.
Thou hast no equal, and thy mind
    Had thoughts as beautiful as psalms;
Each lovely word of thine I find
    My heart with gentlest pleasure calms.

A ROSY FACE AND CHESTNUT HAIR.

A rosy face and chestnut hair
   Beguiled me in the hours of Spring,
No other face I'd seen so fair,
   Ne'er thought so much about a ring!
Would she be mine? ah, would she say—
   Would she but only answer, yes!
I vowed I'd name the marriage day,
   Make one unwedded beauty less!

She shed fresh beauties where she walked,
   Gave brightness to each leafy shade,
To doves on myrtle branches talked,
   And more delight than music made!
Like summer's latest rose her cheek
   The faintest trace of crimson wore,
Words would be poor its charm to speak,
   Of beauty there could not be more!

And fresher lips I ne'er had seen,
    They made enchantment when they stirred,
As sweet before there may have been,
    But none so formed to grace a word!
'T was beautiful to see them part,
    And she, unconscious of her charms,
As babe wrought by the sculptor's art,
    With moonlight gleaming on its arms!

That Spring was loveliest unto me,
    By day and night I lived in dreams;
In what we love we daily see
    Hope cast, like sapphire skies in streams!
I won the maiden's heart to mine;
    Long years have passed and still she's fair;
As freshly yet, as sweetly shine
    Her rosy face and chestnut hair!

IF I SHOULD LEAVE THE EARTH ERE THEE.

If I should leave the earth ere thee,
   I hope to see thee when I 'm gone ;
I would then thou could'st gaze on me,
   My best beloved and faithful one.
For we have loved each other well,
   In hours of sunshine and in shade ;
I would I had the power to tell
   The pleasant memories thou hast made.

If I die first, I hope to live
   Within thy memory—in thy prayers ;
With gladness to thy life I 'd give
   A charm against e'en lightest cares.
Though lone without me by thy side,
   My fondest thoughts should all be thine ;
And in this heart thy form should hide,
   Thy pleasures be as great as mine !

If I die first, I hope my name
    Thou 'lt whisper oft in after years;
The truest sign of love and fame
    Is proved by what the memory wears.
We die not if we live with one
    In thought, in speech, we see no more;
For when the evening's light has gone,
    The scenes remain it glimmered o'er!

If I die first, I only crave
    Among thy treasures to be found,
That thou wilt feel unto my grave
    By sympathy for ever bound!
Death only blinds life for a time;
    The living know the lost one's worth;
The dead one lives a dream sublime,
    Whose mysteries have no place on earth.

AMID THE CLOVER.

We 'll walk amid the clover,
  Where oft the wild bee sips
Pale nectar from the flowers
  Not sweeter than thy lips;
Where birds drink from the brooklets
  That murmur as they flow,
And early bramble blossoms
  In pale pink clusters blow.

In sunshine in the valley,
  Dear maiden, roam with me,
And view the fragrant wild flowers
  Bowed by the loving bee.
There 's music in the meadows
  In morning's balmy hours,
When sighs like cooling perfumes
  Rise from the grass and flowers.

The crab-tree's opening blossoms
   (How pearly, pink, and fair!)
I 'll proudly pluck in masses,
   To wreathe thy glossy hair.
And slowly we will wander,
   To rest beside yon stream
That gushes on in silence
   And seems of clouds to dream!

In woodland and in valley
   Love's truest spirit dwells;
Heard when the low wind whispers
   And chimes the foxglove's bells.
In nature's world, dear maiden,
   Love's simplest lessons lie;
Why not all hearts, like flowers,
   United live and die?

SHE LIVES IN HEAVEN.

She lives in Heaven, too fair for earth,
   Her life with us seemed but a day ;
There are no words to speak the worth
   Of one who passed so soon away.
She walks with angels—she was one ;
   Round every thought she threw a grace ;
Home darkens round us now she's gone,—
   There is no sunshine in the place.

We mourn her loss by night and morn.
   And yet we know regret is vain ;
'T is true that pleasures brightly born
   Oft end in agony and pain.
Death hushed her voice when most we sought
   To guard her life from every care ;
She lives and dwells in every thought ;
   So quickly dead—so deeply fair.

Time cannot bridge the gulf between
    Our present love and past delight;
By memory's aid she 's dimly seen
    Through rare and radiant dreams of night.
Within the mind her love will be
    As marble statue niched in gold;
And though her form we cannot see
    Its likeness memory will hold.

'T is only when some lives are o'er
    We learn their beauty, and we mourn;
Yet souls all beautiful will soar,
    And once again to Heaven return.
And she we loved on earth so well
    We felt had left that higher sphere
But for a moment, and to tell
    That angels sometimes wander here!

WHAT SHALL I DO TO WIN HER HAND?

What shall I do to win her hand?
    I've tried all things in vain;
I've vowed by all things in the land,
    The open sky and plain.
I've told her that my love is deep,
    That idle dreams have past;
That this lone memory will keep
    Her form while life shall last.

She heeds me not, but turns away,
    A sweet smile in her look,
As beautiful as bloom of May
    Shut in a gilded book;
Her charms unclosing one by one
    Whene'er she moves or speaks,
While pale pink hues lie dreaming on
    Her round and peerless cheeks.

In every step there is a grace
    That words could never tell :
Where gleams of Paradise I trace,
    And love's warm glories dwell.
For beauty has a power supreme,
    A spell that never tires,
It tints the splendour of each dream,
    Each true emotion fires.

What must I do to win her hand?
    How shall I fondly plead ?
As bright as sparks of gold in sand
    Her glances heavenward lead.
The cords of this poor heart she thrills,
    I'm bound in slavery's chain,
I've sought her by the lakes and rills,
    But sought and wooed in vain !

MAIDEN BEAUTY.

More gleaming eyes were never seen,
    With love they lighted up her face,
As sunshine stealing o'er a flower
    Half hidden in a shaded place.
She looked as calm as saint at prayer,
    And sang as sweet as birds in dells,
When amorous winds in morning hours
    Toy with the cowslip's perfumed bells.

No marble whiter than her arms,
    Lips ne'er before were seen so sweet,
Their hue was as the scarlet flush
    Of poppies 'mong the dewy wheat.
Grace had its throne upon her brow,
    Love made its heaven within her eyes,
And there it shone as in warm morns
    A drop of dew on violet lies.

Upon her cheeks was placed a bloom
    Like coral tint on ivory thrown,
As though she'd lingered near a rose,
    And each for each had hourly grown!
Her dainty laughter made a sound
    More choice than music's lightest strain,
And when she sang her lips unloosed
    Tones bright as April's sun-lit rain.

Art could not add unto her charms,
    For Nature had defied its aid
By giving grace to all her deeds,
    Proud of the beauty it had made.
And in her heart true kindness dwelt,
    Plain in her every look 't was seen;
Eyes ne'er before beheld a maid
    More worthy to be crowned a queen!

THE OPEN WINDOW.

Against the open window
    We'll sit as evening dies,
The shadow of the yew tree
    Across the pathway lies.
No bird is heard to warble;
    The sun's red orb has gone;
In feeling now our young hearts
    Will vibrate, love, as one.

The wind with gentle cadence
    A lovely murmur makes,
And bows the leaves of lilies,
    The lilac-blossom shakes.
It wantons with the beauty
    That dwells upon thy cheek—
Through the window comes in whispers,
    As though it strove to speak.

Pleased with the charm that lingers
   About thy look of grace—
Of Paradise a picture,
   Seen in the sweetest place!
As melodies from woodlands
   The cool night-breezes swim,
In thy presence there 's no darkness
   And night is never dim.

I love the open window,
   When day has gone to rest,
And the night in sable grandeur
   Unveils her mighty breast.
My thoughts fly from the present
   To days for ever past,
While on the open window
   The young night's charms are cast!

AN EPITAPH.

Here lies a man who loved his country well,
Who laboured for its greatness 'ere he fell;
In youth the hater of each cruel law,
The stubborn foe of every wrong he saw.
His zeal unquenched, though long he toiled in vain,
Without one care the world's applause to gain.
He saw with burning heart his brethren crushed,
He heard their freedom cursed, their yearnings hushed;
And there arose within his valiant mind
A power like thunder driven by the wind—
A hope to raise his prostrate kinsmen's race
Firm and unshaken as a mountain's base.

His gleaming thoughts with earnest words were
    crowned,
While on his work each tyrant ruler frowned.
Yet he was dauntless, and he dared each foe,
His teachings grand as prayers for human woe.
He saw the toiler, and mourned o'er his fate,
Worked for the slave of every trampled state.
He was the scion of a noble line,
Not from the rank where "stars" and
    "garters" shine,
But one of Nature's nobles, Thought's high
    king,
Whose deeds will make the coming ages ring.
'T was he who struck the chords of Freedom's
    lyre,
Woke hope from slumber, and with words of fire,
That played like lightnings, gashing sullen
    skies,
Moved forth the simple, and aroused the wise.
He left a name his country loves—reveres,
His memory washed with sorrow's coldest tears.
A name he's left that centuries cannot dim,
His faultless life his country's fervent hymn;
His deeds will orb the ages yet unborn,
Survive each petty despot's poisoned scorn,
Cut paths of glory that shall lead to power,
And make the poor an everlasting dower.

Sleep on, lost hero! Fame for aye is thine,
High in its radiant niche thy name dost shine;
Few lived so well; thine equal ne'er was met;
O'er realms thy mind has blazed and shall not
    set;
Its strength, its force, o'er calumny shall ride—
Love thrilled thy heart and Freedom was thy
    bride!

A CLEAR BLUE SKY AND GOLDEN MOON.

A clear blue sky and golden moon
   Shone sweetly o'er us as we strayed
To grave of one who died too soon,
   Where figure knelt as though it prayed.
The daisies stood upon the grave,
   The grass was shivering in the breeze.
The winds in sadness seemed to rave,
   And breathe a requiem through the trees.

The form that lay beneath the mound
   Was oft a solace in our woe;
And in her every look we found
   All that of joy we cared to know.
Ah, poor dead lamb! her grave is made
   A secret place to shed our tears;
In Memory's shrine her charms are laid,
   Though life a look of sadness wears.

Her voice no more will fill our ears,
    Soft as the music of a dream;
No longer now her form appears,
    Dear as the sunshine on a stream.
No more her cheeks can charm the rose,
    Her eyes the hyacinths eclipse;
Death never came before to close
    On earth such speaking eyes and lips.

The things she loved neglected lie,
    The paths deserted where she strayed;
The couch on which we saw her die,
    The chamber where she nightly prayed.
In death the beautiful embrace
    The memory with their untold worth;
They leave us lonely, but their grace,
    Transferred to heaven, shines down on earth.

THE VACANT CHAIR.

The vacant chair stands by the fire,
    And those I loved are gone;
This heart in sorrow for the dead
    But feebly flutters on.
The form I loved has passed from earth—
    A creature light as air,
Whose memory evermore will bring
    Love for that vacant chair.

That chair is sacred, for it tells
    In silent hours of night
Of her who dwells in heaven now,
    Robed in immortal light.
This relic of the faded past
    Unto the present bears
The image of departed love,
    And sometimes claims my tears.

Things that belong unto the dead
   With reverence fill my heart,
And play in life's strange scenes betimes
   A calm and solemn part.
A faded flower or holy book
   Brings thoughts too deep to tell ;
And she who perished long ago,
   In memory must dwell.

And life, the contrast here of death,
   The dead one's love embalms ;
As the sublimest thoughts of God
   Lie beautiful in psalms.
The simplest things oft charm the heart-
   A book, a lock of hair ;
And fondest thoughts and dreams may cling
   About a vacant chair !

SONG.

Those chestnut curls, I see them yet,
    Droop brightly down thy cheek,
As beautiful as when we met,
    And I first dared to speak.
I held thy lovely hand in mine,
    Asked thee to name the day;
I thought each moment dawned divine,
    And past like dreams away.

Those chestnut curls have golden hues,
    Untouched, undimmed by time;
Soft as the glow of evening dews
    In some warm flowering clime.
And when the sunset paints the west
    In June's most honeyed hours,
Within this heart thy beauties rest,
    As summer rain in flowers.

Those chestnut curls seem proud to lean
  And tremble o'er thy face,
In tides of radiance, my queen,
  Sweet lovers of thy grace.
Like marble idol seen in dreams
  I view thee when alone;
I see thy cheeks as in cool streams
  Wild roses blush full blown!

THE GLORY OF LABOUR.

Listen, friend, unto my story,
    There's a moral in the crowd,
Higher than the claim to glory,
    In the annals of the proud.
List the earnest strokes of labour,
    As from iron blocks they ring;
See the arms that wield a sabre
    For a country and a king!

In the crowds of workers ever
    There's a lesson for the vain;
On the land its chorus surges
    Loud as storm upon the main.
Knowledge springs from labour's battle
    As the gem comes from the mine;
For its blessings are immortal,
    With its wealth the nations shine.

At the forge brave labour swelters
    In the city's ceaseless hum,
Never flagging, never resting,
    Though oft wearied never dumb!
Stern the spirits that long wrestle
    With the daily cares of life,
With its suffering and its trials,
    And its never vanquished strife.

As I walk among the workers
    Oft my heart with love is filled,
For I know their deeds and courage
    Every throne and country gild!
That the highest and the proudest
    Owe a fealty to the men
Who delve in mine and quarry,
    And to toilers with the pen!

Those rare men who mould our morals
    Set great thoughts in language strong;
Men of every right the lovers
    And the foes of every wrong!
Labour solves the golden secret
    Of old England's wealth and fame
Clasps her brow with gleaming chaplet,
    Stamps with sterling praise her name!

All the greatness of each nation
    From the hand of labour springs ;
Evermore its massive music
    Rolls around the world and rings !
Busy in the mine and mountain,
    Rearing verdure on the sod,
Carving wonders out of nature,
    With the bravery of a god !

TWILIGHT REVERIES.

There is a sadness in the heart
    That comes upon us unawares
That bows the struggling spirit down,
    That ladens life with gravest cares.
The sadness may not haunt us long,
    Yet while it lasts we mourn and pine;
It comes, perchance, that we may see
    Beyond its darkness pleasure shine.

In secret oft we 're made to weep
    When friends around may smile and sing;
Our greatest sorrow sometimes comes
    From heeding not some trifling thing.
While in the distance there may gleam
    A blessing that may cheer us on;
A heart to brave our present ills
    Would soon feel half the burden gone.

Bright days may cheer us for a time
    And moments charm us as they 're born,
Then all their glories turn to tears
    Like rain-drops in the face of morn!
Wherefore these changings of the mind—
    These pleasures that but briefly stay?
These hopes that in the future lie,
    That fade as soon as dying day!

And why these nights of long despair,
    Until the mind is wrapped in gloom?
Perchance the darkest thoughts we feel
    Are gifts that germinate with bloom.
E'en every household has its woe,
    Some relic speaking of the past,
That sends a sorrow through the mind
    Like dead leaf driven by the blast.

It seems poor human nature's lot
    To feel through life some touch of pain—
To struggle through the darkest hours
    And seek for gladness once again.
Life's sum of happiness seems made
    Of luring smiles and many fears,
As truest love is ever made
    Of sweetest laughter and of tears.

AN EVENING SCENE.

All red and warm the setting sun
    Upon the open casement shone,
The clouds with golden tints were touched,
    And to the west went sailing on ;
In at the open casement stood
    Geraniums, bending with their flowers,
Whose leaves looked as though dipped in blood,
    Seen in the evening's dying hours.

No sound was heard, save at the door
    The leaves of chestnut whispering low ;
We saw the sun sink down the west,
    And heard the zephyrs faintly blow ;
They stirred the leaves of gilded book
    Upon the open casement laid,
And with the young geranium flowers
    They softly toyed and calmly played.

A dewy light, like morning mist,
    Swam slowly through the gleaming panes;
No warble came from birds that hid
    'Mong blossoms in the village lanes.
A fountain in the garden played,
    Whose waters fell in murmurous showers,
And near lush honeysuckles trailed,
    Clomb on the roof of secret bowers.

We watched until the sun's red rim
    No longer lingered on our gaze,
While dwelt about the radiant west
    A softly mellow-molten haze.
'T was then the winds came shivering down
    The garden 'tween the orange bloom,
As evening's beauty slowly died,
    And night arose in silent gloom.

The moon one moment lit the scene,
    Peered through the clouds that dimmed the sky,
While near her orb a star would peep
    And twinkle like a laughing eye.
One moment 'bove the fleecy clouds
    The moon would seem to ripple up,
And in the lake her image place,
    Like sun-flushed pearl in crystal cup.

Love grows divine in such sweet hours,
    Upholds its truth and speaks its thought ;
And finds more pleasure when alone
    Than e'er in honeyed dreams was sought ;
And at the open casement oft
    I met my love in summer eves,
When 'tween our whispers only came
    The tender rustling of the leaves.

And when by night the winds have stirred
    The leaves of dark green ivy bowers,
So icy cold the stars have looked
    Throughout the still and happy hours.
Give me the long, long summer nights ;
    The little casement opened wide ;
When all the blushes of my love
    The beauteous night seems proud to hide.

BEAUTY.

Oh! beauty, in thy radiant span
    The universe is laid;
Thou art the dazzling throne of man,
    From sky to emerald glade.
The mirror of that unseen God,
    By sage and poet sought,
The silent crowner of the sod,
    The central throne of thought!

With thee I ever love to roam
    And own thy potent sway,
Thou girdest up the rainbow's home,
    The gorgeous brow of day!
The great and good of every clime
    Thy looks all gracious claim,
With passions earnest and sublime
    As martyr's couch of flame!

BESIDE THE EVENING FIRE.

I sit beside the evening fire
    And view strange pictures of the past,
With that delight that cannot tire,
    That charms betimes while life shall last;
I see the faces of the dead,
    Pale figures of the days no more,
Young friends who briefly lived, then sped
    To join the dead who fell before.

In lonely hours the memory goes
    In search of what we once held dear,
And like a skilful sculptor shows
    Forms of departed ones once near.
And half alive again they seem,
    And smile by fancy's subtle aid,
Till, filled with pleasure, oft we deem
    Death has but partial silence made.

Still gazing in the fire, we see
    The dying embers lick the bars ;
A sign of what our end will be
    Ere souls soar past the far-off stars.
The faces of the first we knew
    Start dimly on the slumbering mind.
Faint as upon the darkened view
    Warm daylight falls on eyes half blind.

Some face we loved more than the rest
    A moment comes, then quickly dies ;
The spot on which the form was prest
    Dies off, and then in ashes lies.
And yet these pictures, in the eve
    Seen in the fire, some knowledge give :
That the departed only leave
    This earth in other spheres to live.

THE MAIDEN'S VOICE.

There is a freshness in her voice
    That wins me to her side ;
For lesser beauty than she owns
    True hearts ere this have died.
Her equal I have never seen ;
    Her heart I cannot reach ;
I tremble as I meet her glance,
    Yet lack the power of speech.

I envy every spot she views ;
    I fain would be her flowers,
Pressed fondly to her dainty lips
    In May's white blossomed hours.
I see a grace in every step ;
    There's magic in her feet ;
She walks the earth as light and calm
    As zephyrs o'er the wheat.

Her beauty realms me every hour;
    Her captive I am made;
There is no shadow where she roams—
    She brightens every shade!
She is not proud, she is not vain—
    But never dare I speak—
Yet were I asked to find a queen
    I know where I should seek!

I 'm bound in slavery day and night,
    And gladly wear the chain;
Its links are gold; I would not break,
    For worlds, one link in twain.
Could I my happy secret tell,
    My hopes might live no more;
But, while the doubt is in my heart,
    The maiden I adore.

IN THE COURTS AND ALLEYS BORN.

In the courts and alleys born,
   Poverty's lean children mourn;
There are hearts with sorrow torn,
   There are brains that ever burn,
      Full of pain,
      Like a chain,
Grasping limbs of slave by night
Till the blood starts into sight.

In these courts and alleys dwell
   Creatures who are born to pine,
Suffering woes they never tell,
   Slaving on in Labour's mine.
      While they tire
      With desire
All in vain for meanest things,
Pained with hunger's torturing stings.

In their homes no gladness wakes,
   Hot tears mount into the eyes,
Each poor life of sadness takes,
   Each poor slave in misery dies;
      Glad to go
      From the woe
He was born to bear on earth
From the moment of his birth.

Darksome, sickening homes they fill,
   Where the sunshine feebly pours;
In midnight slumbers only still,
   Prostrate on the cheerless floors,
      Lost in dreams,
      As in streams
Children lose their treasured toys—
Cares are lost perchance for joys.

Jaded sires and famished maids
   Huddled in a starving mass,
Touched by death the picture fades,
   Ghost-like, into graves they pass;
      And they leave
      Few to grieve
That their days on earth are o'er—
Sad the funerals of the poor.

Pomp sets up no marble bust
    When some humble genius dies,
But he mingles with the dust
    With no tablet where he lies;
        He was poor,
        And no more
Will he write his wants and wrongs,
Ossian-like, in burning songs.

Weary, weary are the hours
    To the poor ones of the land;
Hunger-palsied oft their powers,
    And like skeletons they stand;
        While each face
        Looks the place
Where despair clings solemn—sore,
Carving wrinkles evermore.

Misery writes upon the brow
    Like a carver on a stone;
Poverty the form can bow,
    Ere stern manhood's thoughts are
        Eyes grow dim   [known:
        As they swim
With hot tears, and aching brain
Throbbing loud as falling rain.

Hopes I cherish that a day
   For the poor may yet arise,
When their woes shall pass away,
   Like a storm that slowly dies,
      And no shame
      Tinge the name
Of the toiler through the land,
Working with strong arm and hand.

SITTING AT THE WINDOW.

I was sitting at the window
   With the Lady Geraldine,
On a gleaming eve in summer,
   Brighter I had never seen,—
I was proud as proudest monarch
   Sitting by the fairest queen.

Through the window came the sunlight,
   And we saw the vine-leaves shake,
While the swans were gliding stately
   All about the limpid lake,
And we watched the shining ripples
   By the swans' white bosoms break.

On the lake were opened lilies,
   Which the south wind gently stirred,
With an accent soft and trembling
   As the music faintly heard
In a distant bush of blossoms,
   Made by warblings of a bird.

In the room, upon the pictures
   Did the sunlight warmly stream,
And the statue of a Cupid
   Stood as though in lustrous dream
On a dove of marble gazing
   With a cool and icy gleam.

Then I whispered to the lady,
   And her face was near to mine,
In her eyes of deepest meaning
   Tender pleadings seemed to shine,
Pure as raindrops seen at evening
   On the violet and vine.

Long we whispered of the future,
   Love-thoughts came between each tone,
Beautiful as birds that flutter
   Near us all unseen—unknown,
When the perfumes from the jasmines
   Through the laurel trees are blown.

Oft her brow the lady shaded
   With her little rosy hand,
And her arms, as white as ivory,
   Were each held in golden band;
Curved like young moon were the dimples
   On her round cheeks zephyr-fanned.

Unto me her heart was given
   On that sunny summer day,
Sitting at the open window,
   Where the gentle sunshine lay,
When the clear lake's radiant ripples
   With the young swans seemed to play.

ON THE RIVER.

On the river in the evening
    Soft and fair the ripples float,
And like liquid gold come crowding,
    Breaking round our little boat;
And the willow droops and kisses,
    As a lover, every wave
That leaps up in tiny splendour
    Thymy banks and flowers to lave.

Not a whisper breaks the silence
    Of this evening's waning hour,
And the cooling dews have clustered
    On each leaf and sleeping flower;
Now the opening hawthorn blossoms
    Loose their fragrance to the gale,
And the clouds in stately beauty
    White as snowy mountains sail.

On the stream their forms are lying
    Glowing as they melt away
In the blue and starry distance
    That gleams o'er the perished day;
From our oars the water trickles,
    Mingles with the sleeping tide,
And the stars are throbbing faintly
    Where the sun sank down and died.

There's an odour from the lilacs,
    And the lute is softly blown;
To the wood, its vernal heaven,
    The lorn nightingale has flown;
And we listen to its warblings,
    Poured upon the silent night,
In our boat upon the river
    Gilded with the pale moonlight.

MAIDEN WORSHIP.

I would not fear death's visit, love,
   If I could see thee when I 'm gone,
Behold thee on those pathways rove
   As when, my love, we lived as one;
For I could never love again
   Another form so dear as thine:
When youthful years are on the wane,
   Past pleasures most unclouded shine.

I could gaze on thee night and day,
   As I have done since first we met;
My love, I vow, knows no decay:
   It rose on thee, and ne'er will set.
I'd rarely take my gaze from thee,
   Pleased that earth held one angel guest,
One who on earth was dear to me,
   My first enchantress and the best.

And could I make thy pleasures more,
   Thy life's dear moments on should glide
Still as the waves that kiss a shore
   And die in laughter side by side!
From every care I 'd shield thee well,
   And to thy dreams Love's glories give,
For with me thou wouldst ever dwell,
   And in thy mind I 'd ever live.

As light as whispers from the west,
   First faintly heard in night's calm hours,
I 'd toil to charm thee unto rest,
   Thou queen of all my thoughts and powers.
My pride would be to see thee own
   No rival on the earth to me,
And if my love has purely shone,
   Its truth and beauty sprang from thee.

LITTLE CHERUB.

Little cherub! oh! what wonder
   Beaming in those deep blue eyes;
Lovelier orbs ne'er trembled under,
   Ever shone through laughing skies.
From those eyes there swims a lustre
   Mellow as the glimmering south,
And with love thy dark curls cluster
   Round thy little radiant mouth.

Little cherub! in thy speeches
   I can trace all things divine;
Not one syllable but teaches
   That God's blessings round thee twine.
Every glance gives me a feeling
   Of a holier state than this,
All that's beautiful revealing—
   And what pleasure in thy kiss.

Little cherub! though thou 'rt simple,
    When I touch thy dainty hand,
And gaze on each cheek's pink dimple,
    Nearer Heaven I seem to stand;
For thou knowest not of sorrow
    With thy soul unskilled in guile;
Dreams of love from thee I borrow,
    Nestling in each happy smile.

Little cherub! worlds above me
    I behold when thou art near;
For thy gentle looks I love thee,
    Where sweet Eden-gleams appear.
In thy presence life ne'er darkles—
    Dwells unclouded in thine eye
That sweet light of love that sparkles
    Like a white star in the sky.

Little cherub! o'er thee hover
    Heaven's young angels day and night,
May each lead thee as a lover—
    Ever spread thy path with light;
For thy beauty has embraced me
    With a charm of nameless worth:
If it be that Heaven has graced thee,
    Paradise is linked to earth!

WASTED DAYS.

Our wasted days, oh! where are they?
   Those bright and precious pearls of Time;
Gone to the darkness of the past,
   Like friends lost in a distant clime.
They come no more—those wasted days—
   Fled swift as brightness of a dream,
Gone as the picture of a cloud
   Glassed but one moment in a stream.

'T is from the past we learn our loss
   And see the gifts we 'd fain recall:
Alas! their shadows faintly loom
   And on the mournful present fall.
When flowers are blooming at our feet,
   Unheeded oft we pass them by,
And moments that have golden wings
   We never miss until they fly.

We look into the silent past—
    Dead hopes, dead blessings there we find,
Like fragments of the wildest thoughts
    That throng betimes a broken mind.
Why should we mourn as life declines,
    When all its scenes are nearly o'er?
Youth looks upon the joy to come,
    And Age the joy that comes no more.

One wasted day takes from our life
    A treasure laid within our reach,
The sorrows for its loss too late
    The truest, sternest lessons teach.
Regrets are vain when round us cling
    The sad views of expiring years:
Why tremble when through life's last hours
    The cold white face of death appears?

A DIRGE.

Young maiden, thou hast left the earth,
   Too beautiful thou wast to stay ;
Till now I never knew thy worth—
   We love things most when far away.
This world was all too vain for thee,
   Its cares and strife thou couldst not bear :
Thou wast an angel unto me,
   And now in memory thou art dear.

Thy life but like a moment seemed,
   And I was joyous by thy side,
For o'er my soul thy beauty beamed
   Far too divine for earth to hide.
Thou 'rt gone, and I am left to mourn.
   To walk thy favoured paths alone :
Oh ! madness ! there is no return :
   Bird-like, for ever thou hast flown.

It seems that while we linger here
    Time robs us day by day of charms,
And while some pleasure lingers near,
    Death folds it in his icy arms.
A blessing comes and quickly goes—
    Leaves home like some deserted nest,
And memory clings to where it rose,
    And loves its first great loss the best.

E'en so with thee, my dearest one,
    Thy books neglected round me lie,
I scarce believe that thou art gone,
    So young thou wast to droop and die.
Yet so it is; and I must make
    Thy absence now one source of thought:
In mourning for some loved one's sake
    We learn death tells what life ne'er taught.

THE SLEEPING CHILD.

The child is nestling in its bed,
    And throws about its little arms,
The curls dishevelled on its head
    Add grace unto its tiny charms.
'T is lost to care, it never knew
    The depths of sorrow, for its tears
Last briefer than the morning dew
    The golden-clouded autumn wears.

Now still one moment; while its lips
    Blush deeper than the scarlet flowers;
From pleasure's cup it ever sips,
    As blossoms quaff of April showers;
The world to it is all unknown—
    What cares and sorrows it may meet!
What would I give that I might own
    Some days as glad and nights as sweet.

Her little brow is cool and white,
    The blue veins on its eyelids show
As purest streaks of azure light
    Upon a path of frosted snow.
May angels guard thee, little one,
    From every care and every pain,
And thy dear life, when I am gone,
    Remain as now without a stain!

I ask a blessing for thee, child;
    God grant that thou may'st never find
One hour when thou wilt be beguiled
    To deeds that show a fallen mind.
I could gaze on thee till hot tears
    Unbidden to these eyes would start:
Asleep, I see thy nature wears
    The beauty that transcends all art.

THE VILLAGE AT EVENING.

The villagers have left the church,
　Whose tall and mouldering spire
Stands in the sunset's dying gleam,
　Like column fixed in fire.
The yew-tree there as mourner stands,
　Each branch a sable shroud,
Perchance thrown o'er the mingled graves
　Of men once gay and proud.

The shadows of the solemn elms
　Across the churchyard lie,
And clouds, white as the angels' feet,
　In groups dissolve and die.
The faintest breeze the poplar stirs,
　Whose leaves it slowly turns;
The young grass trembles; while the west
　Fire-robed and cloud-thronged burns.

Day's orb has gone, and in the lanes
    The air is cool and sweet,
And whispers soft as sighs of love
    Come from the shivering wheat.
As bells of silver lightly rung,
    The rill its music makes,
And from the quiet scene the heart
    A nameless blessing takes.

The light has wandered from the banks,
    The day has folded up
Its volumed beauty, like a gem
    Shut in an ebon cup;
And lulled in peace the village seems,
    The birds and bees are still,
The only sound that tells of life
    Breaks from the murmuring rill.

BACCHANALIAN.

Now from the silver goblets quaff
    Red wine—the merry wine;
At care and sorrow let us laugh—
    Flame-like the tankards shine.
We'll drink to all good hearts that beat
    To aid each noble plan;
While at the festive board we meet
    We're brothers, man to man.

See how the wine-beads bubble up
    The goblet's gleaming sides:
The red wine in the amber cup
    Fill up in crimson tides.
Quaff to each maiden's beauty now,
    For beauty is our theme,
For maids who love us breathe a vow—
    The wine-sparks redly beam.

THE STORM.

By night I listened to the storm,
   I heard it strike the trees,
It sounded like the sullen roar
   From organ's deep bass keys.
The rain fell pattering in the street
   And down the gutters ran :
I thought it seemed like to the tears
   That splash the earth from man.

One moment and the storm was dumb,
   Then loud again it broke,
The cottage shook, the huge trees groaned.
   Beneath its god-like stroke ;
The sky was sable ; on the moor
   Down dashed the rain in lines ;
The brooklet roared, the river writhed,
   Like black plumes waved the pines.

In blinding grandeur lightnings leapt
    And gashed the murky sky;
One moment calm, and then the wind
    In howling strains rushed by.
I thought how puny were man's deeds,
    And yet how loud his boast,
How poor his pride when ocean sings
    Hoarse anthems to the coast.

I love, when storms the forests strike,
    To list them madly race,
To hear the winds make cities shake
    With their unequalled bass.
When thunders roll like gods aroused,
    I gladly hail the strain;
While northern gales with furious clash
    Wring music from the rain.

IN HER LONE ROOM.

In her lone room dwelt the maiden,
   And her cheeks were wet with tears,
Though her heart with love was laden
   All her thoughts were tinged with fears;
Then she looked out from the casement,
   But no gladness lit her eye:
Gazed she till the day had vanished—
   Left to earth a darkened sky.

For the one she loved had fallen,
   Perished in his country's name,
And his deeds had borrowed lustre
   From the mighty voice of fame.
Long she 'd waited for his coming,
   Waited till her heart grew faint,
Till she looked as white and speechless
   As a newly-sculptured saint.

And another sought to clasp her,
    But her heart was dead to him;
Scenes before that looked the gayest
    Were no more—the future dim.
Not a smile e'er lit her feature,
    Pleasures from her mind had flown,
Withered, and were lost for ever,
    Like the leaves from dead tree blown.

Day by day her brow grew paler,
    And the power of thought was o'er,
Same as sudden pause in music
    Whose vibrations live no more.
Near the village church she slumbers,
    Angel, while she lived, of love;
Now the earth holds but the mortal—
    The immortal is above.

THE VILLAGE SCHOOL.

Here stands the old school in the lane,
    Here runs the little brook,
Here stands the church with crumbling fane.
    Hard by yet builds the rook.
Long years have gone since last I sped
    Along this ancient way;
The living tell me who are dead,
    The old, and those once gay.

The village green again I pace,
    And view its quiet homes,
I see upon each living face
    Where Age like warrior roams.
I trace a wrinkle on the brow,
    A dimness in the eye,
I see how surely time can bow
    Our forms before they die.

I mark the house, long old and quaint,
    Where my first years were spent,
Upon the mind old memories paint
    The charms each moment lent.
There was no sorrow in my heart,
    No care dwelt in it then,
I thought the earth was but a part
    Of Heaven—its angels men!

I've lived to learn such thoughts were vain,
    For ever they are gone,
I feel that life has much of pain
    When manhood's years come on.
That village school yet looks the same,
    And yet how changed my lot,
Within its walls my errors came,
    And yet I love the spot.

In morning, when the sunset gushed
    In at the open door,
The dim old diamond panes were flushed,
    White radiance splashed the floor.
And jasmines on the window grew,
    Round crumbling walls they ran,
To hide decay, as Heaven, still true,
    Would shield the crimes of man.

THE WORKER.

I wonder when I look around
   Why man should crush his fellow-man;
The earnest toiler, labour-browned,
   Has suffered since the world began,
And those made wealthy by his skill
   But rarely heed his many woes;
And yet what grandeur in his will:
   What thanks to him each nation owes!

I look around, where proudly stand
   His noble works, proof of his worth,
The marvels of his brain and hand
   Are fixed like wonders on the earth;
I see him suffer, and I mourn;
   I love his patience, when his heart,
Perchance like some half-shattered urn,
   With one more touch would break apart.

And from his labour Genius stares,
    Full-eyed, as some large marble god;
I love him when his spirit dares
    To lift the rock, to plough the sod.
In every age, in every clime,
    His stalwart deeds the eye can trace:
Deeds that all symbol the sublime
    And glorify his mighty race.

Upon the sea his works arise,
    On every land through which we roam,
The spires that point up to the skies,
    The cottage, and the marble dome.
I wonder why he's doomed to pine—
    The architect of wealth and fame:
E'en while his works through kingdoms shine
    He dies unwept, without a name!

THE BRIDGE.

Oft upon this bridge I 've wandered
   When the day has gone to rest,
And I 've seen the river darkling,
   With no wave upon its breast ;
I have seen the tall elms mirrored
   In the river's lucent deeps,
Where the morning's first glance glimmers,
   Where the evening's last beam sleeps.

On this bridge I 've stood by midnight,
   Musing o'er this world of strife,
On the strange and wondrous drama
   Of the toiler's lowly life ;
I have pictured on the river
   Oft the faces of the poor,
Deeply scarred and carved with wrinkles,
   Doomed to wear a smile no more.

I've compared the peace of midnight
    To the jars of human crowds,
To the battles of the living
    To the dead in whitened shrouds,
To the sounds of joy and sorrow
    Ever mingling in our ears;
To the moments that bring gladness,
    To the hours made dim with tears.

On this bridge I've sought a solace,
    For I've heard no human sound,
I have felt my spirit hallowed,
    And the fairest blessings found.
With calm ripples on the river
    Gleaming as they glided on,
Breaking into liquid laughter,
    Seen but faintly ere they're gone.

I have pondered on the future,
    Looked with sadness on the past,
Like cloud-shadows on the river
    Felt my hopes in darkness cast,
That the noblest ones should suffer,
    And life's greatest burdens bear:
Yet, oh! peaceful as this river
    May man's future life appear.

RURAL SKETCH.

Above the corn-fields sings the lark,
Soaring towards the azure arc
    Of Heaven on outstretched wings;
And floating smoothly as a bark,
    Aloud his carol rings.

Cool showers have fallen on the grass;
The round drops glimmer as we pass
    On every quivering blade;
The golden lupins in a mass
    Tassel the vernal glade.

There's fragrance from the flowering beans;
Like timid maid the wild rose leans
    With bosom near the rill
That gambols on 'mid sylvan scenes,
    And sings by wooded hill.

The odours from ungathered hay
Are riper than the sighs of May,
    When ruddiest blossoms blow;
In whose sweet deeps at close of day
    Rain drops rose-tinted glow.

The corn is rustling zephyr stirred,
And in the sloe-bush sings a bird
    To charm his silent mate;
Love-voices at the stile are heard,
    And at the rustic gate.

The crimson and white clover flowers
Exhale their sweets at evening hours
    Adown the village lane;
And shadows stripe like fairy towers
    The upland and the plain.

And now the yellow woodbine swings,
One drop of rain the brooklet rings
    With ripples swept from spray
Of bramble; eve's last lustre brings
    The twilight's sober ray.

Now steeped in gold the western skies,
Unsunned the earth flower laden lies
    Like an opulent bride,
While clouds like marble mountains rise,
    And through night's star-gulfs ride.

No shadows linger on the plain,
Bees hum no longer in the lane—
    There broods a mighty calm ;
As when in some cathedral wane
    The last notes of a psalm !

THE BROKEN HARP.

Untouched within my chamber
   The broken harp now stands
Beside a marble figure
   With clapsed and upraised hands.
Its music oft I 've listened
   Till tears would freely start
From the secret founts of sorrow
   Long hidden in the heart.

Like heart too early broken,
   That harp a symbol seems;
It lent a plaintive glory
   To all life's mingled themes.
I 've heard it in the evening,
   Hung o'er it in the morn,
Beheld its bright cords quiver
   As each soft note was born.

Its melting tones have ended,
   Its cadence comes no more
Upon the dying sunshine
   As in the days of yore.
Its strings of golden lustre
   Would shiver at my touch
Like unseen cords that tremble
   In heart that loves too much.

The harp now old and broken
   Sad music yet will make,
Still on my dreams its sweetness
   In plaintive whispers break.
Yet in the quiet evening
   Strains vibrate in my ears,
The sound swims o'er me calmly—
   Falls silently as tears.

The music that we worship
   With passion never dies;
It floats in viewless splendour
   From earth up through the skies.
A tone once struck for ever
   In fancy may be heard,
And in the heart it slumbers
   Hushed as a dreaming bird.

This harp within my chamber,
    Though all its power has gone,
I reverence as a treasure,
    The best and dearest one.
This idol though long broken
    Tells of the bliss it gave,
When memory lies as tranquil
    As sea without a wave!

BESIDE THIS BROOK.

Beside this brook, in days gone by,
    Dear maiden, first we met,
The evening star rose in the sky
    To gem night's coronet!
And from the present to the past
    In sorrow now I look
Upon the joys that could not last
    Beside that singing brook.

Thus memory lingers round the spot
    Where first the heart was won,
Brings back the charms long years forgot,
    Reveals what time has done.
And earliest pleasures broken lie,
    That spot is now forsook
Where I felt love's enslaving tie,
    Dear maid, beside the brook.

FLORENCE NIGHTINGALE.

Sing we of that gifted lady
    Who has shown us noble deeds,
Of her fondness and her daring
    Each true patriot Briton reads.
See her walk among the dying
    With the lamp light in her hand;
See her by the bleeding soldier
    Like a saint in sadness stand.

Hear ye not her voice at even
    Mingling with men's dying moans,
Like the music of a brooklet,
    Charming ears with silver tones?
See her touch the pale, cool temples
    Of the soldier as he lies
On his bed, of England dreaming,
    Angel-tended, ere he dies.

Florence Nightingale! for ever
    Will the name in history bear
An undying hue of splendour,
    Live a deathless idol there.
She, the gracious lady, seeing
    There were sufferings to heal,
Open-hearted, wandered fearless,
    Mercy's mandates to reveal.

In the dim and cheerless winter
    She walked near the glorious dead;
In her gaze the bleeding soldiers
    Saintly love and kindness read.
Round her brow the laurel glistens,
    For her matchless mission done;
Brighter name the bravest hero
    Ne'er deserved and never won.

Through lone passages by midnight,
    When dear lives were ebbing fast,
Then was seen her graceful shadow
    On the bare walls dimly cast;
By the flickering of the lamplight,
    Watching by each hero's bed,
Leaning o'er the gory pillows
    Of the dying and the dead.

MY COUNTRY.

I love my country and my Queen;
   I love the laws by which we live;
The freedom that Old England owns
   To other states I'd freely give.
Old England, there is in thy name
   A magic that no tongue can speak,
And as we dwell upon thy fame
   Pride sets a blush upon the cheek.

Through every clime thy strength is known,
   And who shall dare thy mighty arm?
For where thy regal voice is heard
   Dumb slavery's thrilled as with a charm.
Thy Sovereign fears no frantic cry
   From millions by oppression bound,
But cities with her praises ring,
   With love her throne is girded round.

Through India's burning, bright domain
   Each ruler well her valour knows,
Through regions of eternal ice,
   Her greatness like a triumph goes ;
O'er every sea her worth has gone,
   Her power is known through every land,
Beside her rich heroic realm
     Crowned tyrants shamed and humbled
       stand.

Her people's love is deep and strong :
   Upon their rights she never frowned ;
A liberal heart the best adorns
   Names of the uncrowned and the crowned.
Long live, Old England, thy great Queen ;
   God guard her life from every care ;
For there are swords to shield her throne,
   If e'er a foe that throne should dare.

THE BATTLE OF BOSWORTH.
1485.

The sullen Richard lay and dreamed
    Of Bosworth's bold and bloody fight;
The gore of Richmond on him streamed,
    He struck to earth his bravest knight.
'T was but a dream that broke the rest
    That Richard long and vainly sought;
Upon his steed, with steel-clad breast,
    To hold the crown he fiercely fought.

Wild demons round him howled and danced,
    The ghosts of murdered princes came,
His charger wild with terror pranced,
    His visor hid his look of shame.
His knights and bowmen loudly cheered,
    His steed the frantic monarch spurred,
His hosts the noble Richmond feared,—
    The shouts for victory loud he heard.

He won his right to keep the crown—
    'T was but a dream—delusive scene;
Upon his brow was set a frown,—
    He woke—the combat had not been !
Soon o'er the hills the morning burst
    And flung its splendour on the plain :
The king, for Richmond's blood athirst,
    Must conquer or lie with the slain.

And now is heard the clash of arms,
    And blood for kingly gain is spilt,
The throne for Richard swells with charms.
    The royal gamester red with guilt.
But friendship swerves from Richard's side,
    Crowned or discrowned his reign is o'er,
With crimes thick on his soul he died
    Uncared for, weltering in his gore.

Thus perished greatness based on deeds
    Of coldest murder in the land,
And dark the tragic history reads—
    A stained record must ever stand !
A king of any line or clime
    Who soars to power through blood and
        tears,
Should learn that justice grows sublime
    And hurls to earth the crown he wears.

THE PAST.

Long cherished dreams linked to the past
    Come o'er me as I muse alone;
I see dead pleasures round me cast,
    Like petals from young blossoms blown.
I see the paths where I have strayed
    In quest of joys that could not last;
In vain to hold those joys I 've prayed,—
    Those sweet memorials of the past.

They 're gone like dream that comes no more,
    Gone same as cloud one moment seen;
Now from those long lost days of yore
    I learn how bright the past has been.
I 've learnt that youth 's the time to love,
    The time when earth seems strewn with flowers;
When thoughts, in happiest visions rove,
    And life feels not the fleeting hours.

I might have done some noble deed,
  · Perchance, in days now long gone by;
Have often helped a friend in need,
    And chased the teardrop from the eye.
I look along the silent past,
    And there I see in ruins piled
The hopes too frail and dear to last
    That pleased and cheered me when a child.

Through memory's vista now I see
    Where oft in blindness I have erred;
Forgiveness, God, I ask of Thee,
    For all my crimes—each angry word.
We learn to-day from yesterday
    The strength or weakness of the mind;
The precious gifts we 've thrown away,
    Whose like we ne'er again may find.

The past is like a path that gives
    A glimpse of flowers on either side;
We feel that each no longer lives;
    And date the hours when each one died.
E'en as when day has closed and gone,
    And glided grandly from our view,
We see the spot on which it shone
    Without one brightened tint or hue.

AUTUMN.

High up the whitened fire of morn
    A lark sprang from a wood,
And o'er the fields of ripened corn
    His notes fell in a flood.
Old Autumn, like a sun-browned Queen,
    Blessed earth with kisses cold;
Hedges had lost their glossy green,
    And looked like paths of gold.

Ripe berries hung in rubied crowds
    On loose and graceful stems;
The nights came forth unmarred with clouds,
    Most luminous with gems.
The moon in her blue palace stood,
    And silvered hill and plain,
The trees' dim shadows from the wood
    Lay down like giants slain.

I love old Autumn's lustrous eves,
   Its cold and keen bright hours,
Its loads of brown and fallen leaves,
   Its midnight splendour—showers ;
Its crimson pathways in the west,
   Its blaze on sea and land,
Its proud sun, Heaven's most gorgeous guest,
   Its round fruits juiced and tanned !

TREAD SLOWLY.

Tread slowly in the chamber dim,
   For there our little darling lies;
And in her sleep she sings a hymn
   Whose music low and liquid dies.
We 've watched for days above her bed;
   Through weary nights afraid to speak;
So still she 's lain we 've thought her dead,
   A marble whiteness on each cheek.

Our hope betimes has made us vain
   That she would live, and then our fears
Have filled our hearts with grief again—
   Unlocked the secret fount of tears.
Wealth had no charm for us so sweet
   As her dear life, for she was one
Whose form we ever joyed to meet,
   Missed like lost jewel now she 's gone.

She passed from earth, and downward fell
    The deepest gloom upon our lives ;
Robbed of a pleasure loved too well.
    Despair the memory madly dives.
Now our dead darling fills a place
    In life's dark annals that shall last ;
'T is death's record of perished grace—
    A still memorial of the past.

One life beloved that daily gives
    Its gladness to increase our own.
Tells that in human nature lives
    More mystery than the wise have shown.
And our lost treasure, though no more
    She charms us with her tiny speech,
Is lovely now as when before
    She closed her eyes on us—on each !

FANCIES.

Let me hear the south winds blow
   O'er violets dew-drop laden,
Let me hear the brooklet flow
   And laugh like love-charmed maiden;
Bring me shells from ocean's deeps,
   With hues all faint and pearly,
Like the tint that lightly sleeps
   In blossoms opening early.

Bring me cups of coral, filled
   With dew from pale primroses,
Let me see the sunset gild
   The river as eve closes;
'Mong wild woodbines let me rest,
   To sounds of zephyrs listen,
When about the sunless west
   The stars arise and glisten.

"LEOLINE; AND LYRICS OF LIFE."

BY

S. H. BRADBURY (QUALLON).

OPINIONS OF THE PRESS.

From the Times.

In speaking of Mr. Bradbury's first volume, "Edenor, a Dramatic Poem, and Miscellaneous Lyrics," *The Times* said: "The author is simple, natural, and poetical. 'By the by,' Southey wrote to Coleridge, 'there is a great analogy between hock, claret, pork pie, and the Lyrical Ballads. Wordsworth's are asparagus and artichokes, good with plain butter, and wholesome.' So we say of Mr. Bradbury's lyrics. They are thoroughly digestible without pepper. A homely freshness breathes from the leaves. They smell of the garden. Read these lines to *Little Mary*, and say if they be not worth a wardrobe of theatrical feathers, red mantles, and paint, or a whole ream of Pindarics? . . . . . Let 'Quallon' remember that sweet bird which is always dropping to earth even in the midst of his song. The home affections never defraud the singer. If he will celebrate these we shall expect him to be satisfied with his reward. He will paint them well because he feels them."

Morning Post.

"Parts of Leoline, for instance, are really good."

Literary Gazette.

"Mr. Bradbury displays a real power of catching and photographing the various aspects of nature . . . . and we have seldom read any piece of the same kind with much more pleasure than the following. . . . . Some of the expressions in this Winter Scene are of uncommon excellence . . . are lines which all betray the hand of a true poet. The last stanza is really very fine."

The Critic.

"It is because some, if not all, of those conditions have been followed by Mr. Bradbury, that we have frequently placed him, and still place him, among our best lyrists. . . . . We should not be far wrong if we were to say that 'Leoline' is the most tenderly sweet poem that ever Mr. Bradbury has penned. The opening stanzas effectually conceal the labours of the poet, while they display exquisite nicety of art, and the triple rhymes glide into their places like 'stringed pearls.' . . . . The delicious melody which 'Leoline' as a poem possesses. . . . . . The more we dip into this poem, 'Leoline,' the more we discover objects of beauty."

Standard.

"Mr. Bradbury is well known to the public under the signature of 'Quallon,' and has attained a popularity which the present volume is likely considerably to increase. . . . . 'Labour's Kings' is a heart-stirring lyric."

Morning Herald.

"We cannot withhold our acknowledgment of his vigour, freshness, brilliant fancy, and exceeding sweetness."

Nonconformist.

"He has written pleasing lyrics with much actual feeling and fancy. . . . . A great part of its verse is musical; and its sentiment is warm and true."

News of the World.

"A new volume of poems by Mr. Bradbury is always a subject of interest to the literary world. . . . . . It is this 'freshness' of spirit, which is but another term for originality, in which Mr. Bradbury writes, that has won for him the popularity which he enjoys. . . . . The marvellous imagery with which this is accomplished is matter of astonishment. . . . . Here is a true poet. . . . . It is a book of beautiful poetry, and its originality will secure its permanent attraction."

Daily Telegraph.

"Mr. Bradbury is a self-taught man. All honour to him for the energy by which he has raised himself from a very humble position to rank and standing as a writer."

Northampton Herald.

"The story of 'Leoline' is very beautiful, the composition of it being distinguished by a freshness and purity of style seldom now seen, while many of the 'Lyrics of Life' are charming poems.

Era.

"He has fought his way to the poet's name through difficulties which would have completely overwhelmed and disheartened any but a most devoted worshipper of the Muses. . . . . His poems are melodious and sweet. . . . . He has risen from the ranks with credit to himself, and he has met with friends in high places."

Manchester Examiner and Times.

"Several of the stanzas have a fair claim in 'Leoline' to be ranked among the beautiful, for we find in them feeling which is higher than mere fancy. . . . . . There are verses scattered throughout the volume which show the writer to possess some intimate relation with the true spirit, while they give hope for future advancement in his literary career."

Bristol Mirror.

"Mr. Bradbury will be better known even yet. . . . May he long live, say we, to lift the weeds from life's highway, and exhibit to us the violets that grow beneath. . . . . Here is a specimen of 'Leoline.' . . . . The 'Lyrics of Life' are marked by considerable vigour. Full of rich metaphor and bold imaginings, they abound with gems of thought."

Liverpool Albion.

"They evince considerable imaginative power. In 'Leoline' the captivating qualities of innocence blended with beauty are well depicted. . . . . They breathe manly sentiments."

Derby Mercury.

"'Leoline' is redundant with sweetness, and many of its stanzas are very beautiful. . . . . These are fresh and sparkling, beautiful as true, and invested with the peculiar grace which is characteristic of the author. As a lyric poet Mr. Bradbury is always genial and happy, an irresistible charm pervades his compositions."

Dorset County Chronicle.

"'Leoline' exhibits much true poetical genius; the diction is eloquent, and the tone pure. . . . . Here are his musings over the cradle of the angel child, 'Leoline.' . . . . Here, too, is a charming little bit, which makes us believe that Paradise is not lost to us. . . . . 'Reveries,' and some others, are really beautiful."

Leamington Courier.

"That this new volume of poems abounds with beauties which will render it a permanent source of intellectual pleasure must be universally admitted."

Derby Reporter.

"Passages the book does contain of exceeding beauty, and we conceive equal in character to those penned by any poet of the present day. . . . . We have rarely met with a sweeter photograph than the following of the lineaments of a lovely, light-hearted, cheerful child. . . . . . After reading the foregoing passages who shall question the remark that Bradbury is a poet, and a poet too of no common order?"

Brighton Gazette.

"'Quallon,' the author of 'Yewdale,' 'The Bridal of the Lady Blanche,' and a collection of spirited and musical miscellaneous poems, may be reckoned among the promising young poets of the present day. . . . His poems are vivacious, natural, and flowing; his imagery natural and unstrained, and he has a keen perception of the beautiful in nature. . . . We note the beauty and variety of the images generally employed. We subjoin a few. . . . 'Leoline' . . . is full of beautiful language."

Birmingham Journal.

"His poems are worthy of much praise . . . . he has at his command good nervous language, and considerable powers of illustration. . . . The majority of readers will like the volume, and its love songs will find many readers."

Nottingham Review.

"Mr. Bradbury requires no introduction to our readers. Under the *nom de plume* of 'Quallon' he has again and again sung some of the sweetest melodies of the age. The volume of poetry which he now presents to the public is in all respects worthy to be ranked with those earliest efforts, which have won for him the approbation of the great and the loving admiration of the many."

Leicester Journal.

"If he will persevere in the path he has chosen, with due diligence, we do not despair of his attaining a very high place among the lyric poets of England."

Oxford University Herald.

"Mr. Bradbury will add immensely to his reputation by the principal poem in this volume. . . . Mr. Bradbury is one who thinks like a poet, and works like an artist. . . . Many of the lines are of peculiar beauty."

Leicestershire Mercury.

"Mr. Bradbury has proved that his poetic power is of that sterling kind which gathers strength from years and experience. In almost every page we find some graceful image—some truthful thought—some touch of deep and tender feeling."

Poetical Souvenir.

"Among the poets of the present, perhaps there are few who have so well sustained their reputation, or whose sweet snatches of song have become so generally admired as those of Mr. S. H. Bradbury, who under the *nom de plume* of 'Quallon' has written some of the most musical lyrics in the language.

www.ingramcontent.com/pod-product-compliance
Lightning Source LLC
Chambersburg PA
CBHW031729230426
43669CB00007B/295